AN INTRODUCTION TO TORT-BASED HEALTHCARE LITIGATION

Caldwell G. Collins and
Robert A. Chu, Editors

AMERICAN BAR ASSOCIATION
Litigation Section

Cover design by Jill Tedhams/ABA Design

Printed in the United States of America.

25 24 23 22 21   5 4 3 2 1

Library of Congress Cataloging-in-Publication Data

Names: Collins, Caldwell G., editor. | Chu, Robert A., editor.
Title: An introduction to tort-based healthcare litigation / Caldwell G. Collins and Robert A. Chu, editors.
Description: Chicago, Illinois : ABA Publishing, American Bar Association, [2021] | Includes index. | Summary: "An Introduction to tort-based health care litigation in collaboration with Health Law Committee of the American Bar Association's Section of Litigation"—Provided by publisher.
Identifiers: LCCN 2020057823 (print) | LCCN 2020057824 (ebook) | ISBN 9781641057974 (paperback) | ISBN 9781641057981 (ebook)
Subjects: LCSH: Medical personnel—Malpractice—United States—Trial practice.
Classification: LCC KF8925.M3 I58 2021 (print) | LCC KF8925.M3 (ebook) | DDC 344.7304/11—dc23
LC record available at https://lccn.loc.gov/2020057823
LC ebook record available at https://lccn.loc.gov/2020057824

This book is dedicated to
Christy Tosh Crider, who taught
Editor Collins the practice of—and
more importantly, the passion for—
healthcare litigation.

Contents

Chapter 2

Common Issues in Long-Term Care Litigation

Caldwell G. Collins and Brittany Bartley Simpson

Chapter 3

Pharmaceutical Product Liability Litigation

Tamar Kelber and Daniel Kennedy

Chapter 4

Medical Device Litigation: Theories of Liability and Common Defenses

Samuel L. Felker and Sarah Murray

Chapter 5

Statutes of Limitation, Tolling, Tort Damage Caps, Certificates of Medical Merit, and Venue

James Bush

Chapter 6

Privilege

Jacqueline Promislo

Chapter 7

The Recovery of Damages in Healthcare Tort Actions

Janelle L. Davis and John P. Atkins

Chapter 8

Experts

Kimberly Grant Silvus

PREFACE

This book represents the collaborative effort of the Health Law Committee of the American Bar Association's Section of Litigation. The Committee is dedicated both to the development of health law and to educating its members about best practices in litigating health law claims. The Committee conceived this book as a practical guide for lawyers who are either beginning a health law practice or handling a health law case in an unfamiliar area. This book does not assume that the reader is on either side of "the v." Instead, it is written to provide guidance regardless of which party the reader represents. While there are many topics that are not covered in this book, the Committee believes it is a good place to start. We hope you agree.

The opinions expressed in this book are those of the authors alone and are not necessarily the opinions or positions of their firms or their clients. Similarly, authors' statements should not be taken as legal advice, and if a reader is seeking legal advice, the reader should reach out to a lawyer—including any of the authors—directly.

Acknowledgments

The editors wish to acknowledge the chapter authors and American Bar Association editors, without whose hard work and dedication this book would not exist, as well as Aaron Krauss, Sam Felker, Nash Long, and Maura Monoghan, who encouraged the authors to write the book and provided guidance on how to do so.

The editors also wish to acknowledge Jenni Allison: this book would not have been possible without her hard work, selfless dedication, and countless editing hours.

About the Contributors

Chapter 1

Nicole DeMaise is General Counsel, Vice President of Legal and Compliance at DemystData in New York, New York. Ms. DeMaise has represented clients on a full range of medical malpractice issues. Her practice also encompasses matters relating to complex commercial litigation, intellectual property litigation, product liability, premises liability, construction defects, insurance coverage disputes, and appellate issues. Ms. DeMaise received her law degree from Rutgers School of Law–Camden, with high honors, in 2003 and her undergraduate degree from Rutgers College in 2000. After graduating law school, she served as law clerk for the Honorable Francine I. Axelrad, New Jersey Superior Court, Appellate Division. Ms. DeMaise was named a *New Jersey Super Lawyer®* Rising Star in 2014.

Leslie Isaacman Yohey is an attorney in the healthcare litigation group at Baker, Donelson, Bearman, Caldwell & Berkowitz, PC, in Memphis, Tennessee. She represents and counsels healthcare clients in a wide range of litigation, compliance, and regulatory matters. Ms. Yohey received her law degree in 2009 from the University of Memphis, where she was the managing editor for the *Tennessee Journal of Practice and Procedure* and served on the Moot Court Board. She received her undergraduate degree from Rhodes College in 2004, and she received her MBA from Christian Brothers University in 2014. In her spare time, Ms. Yohey engages in pro bono work, and she serves on the boards of the Hagar Center and Mid-South Spay and Neuter Services.

Sarah Pazar Williams is an attorney with Hall Booth Smith, PC, in Memphis, Tennessee. She specializes in healthcare liability, medical malpractice, nursing home and long-term care defense, general liability, and premises liability litigation. Ms. Williams received her law degree from Vanderbilt Law School, where she served as Chief Justice of the Moot Court Board and the Executive Development Director of the *Vanderbilt Journal of Transnational Law*. Ms. Williams has served as the chair of the Young Lawyers' Committee of Memphis Area Legal Service's Campaign for Equal Justice since 2014. Prior to law school, Ms. Williams attended Northwestern University and worked in the nonprofit sector in Chicago. She is the proud founder of Northwestern University's Memphis Club.

Chapter 2

Caldwell G. Collins, a shareholder in the Nashville office of Baker, Donelson, Bearman, Caldwell & Berkowitz, PC, leads the firm's Long-Term Care Litigation group. She advises healthcare providers in professional liability actions, payor disputes, government investigations, and daily operational challenges. Ms. Collins is a graduate of Washington University in St. Louis School of Law, where she was Editor-in-Chief of the *Washington University Journal of Law & Policy*, president of the Women's Law Caucus, and recipient of the Association of Women Faculty Graduate Student Award. Ms. Collins received her BA in English literature from Vanderbilt University. In 2018, she was named an "On the Rise—Top 40 Young Lawyer" by the American Bar Association; she was selected as a fellow of the Nashville Bar Foundation in 2020; and she has been listed as a Mid-South Rising Star by *Super Lawyers Magazine* each year since 2014.

Brittany Bartley Simpson is an attorney with Baker, Donelson, Bearman, Caldwell & Berkowitz, PC. She represents clients in business-related litigation, healthcare litigation, and entertainment law matters. Mrs. Simpson graduated from the University of Mississippi School of Law, summa cum laude, where she was the Executive Editor of the *Mississippi Law Journal*'s online companion. While in law school, Mrs. Simpson served as an intern for the U.S. District Court of the Eastern District of Tennessee for the Honorable Thomas A. Varlan. In addition, she was a legal extern at the Volunteer Lawyers and Professionals for the Arts located in Nashville, Tennessee. Mrs. Simpson received her BBA from Belmont University.

Chapter 3

Tamar Kelber is a member with Gass Weber Mullins LLC in Milwaukee, Wisconsin. She has represented pharmaceutical manufacturers in products liability litigation since 1995 and represents a wide range of clients in commercial cases. Ms. Kelber received her law degree from Northwestern University School of Law, where she was Associate Articles Editor of the *Northwestern Law Review*. After graduating from law school, she served as a law clerk for Judge James B. Loken, U.S. Court of Appeals for the Eighth Circuit. Before joining Gass Weber Mullins LLC, Ms. Kelber was an associate and partner at Sidley Austin LLP in Chicago, Illinois. She has served as cochair of the ABA Pharmaceutical, Medical Device and Biotech Product Liability Subcommittee and chaired the ABA Current Issues in Pharmaceutical and Medical Device Litigation Seminar in 2013 and 2014.

Daniel Kennedy is an attorney with Gass Weber Mullins LLC in Milwaukee, Wisconsin. Mr. Kennedy has represented businesses and individuals in products liability, commercial, and other civil litigation matters since 2006. Mr. Kennedy received his law degree, summa cum laude, from the University of Illinois College of Law, where he served on the Editorial Board of the *University of Illinois Law Review*. Following graduation, Mr. Kennedy served as a law clerk to Chief Judge Barbara B. Crabb, U.S. District Court for the Western District of Wisconsin.

Chapter 4

Samuel L. Felker is a shareholder in the Nashville office of Baker Donelson Bearman Caldwell & Berkowitz, PC, and focuses his litigation practice on the defense of product liability, food safety, mass torts, and commercial cases. In pharmaceutical and medical device litigation, Mr. Felker has served as national, regional, and local counsel in defending manufacturers throughout the United States. During the course of his career, he has also represented clients in significant commercial litigation involving insurance coverage, securities fraud, breach of contract, theft of trade secrets, defamation, and intellectual property. Mr. Felker currently serves as Cochair of the ABA Section of Litigation Products Liability Committee and Chair of the Metro Nashville Board of Health.

Sarah Murray is an attorney with Baker Donelson, Bearman, Caldwell & Berkowitz, PC, in Nashville, Tennessee. Ms. Murray represents clients in various business litigation matters. She graduated from Vanderbilt University School of Law, where she was the Executive Student Editor of the *Vanderbilt Journal of Transnational Law* and received the John A. Cortner Championship Award for winning the 2013 Vanderbilt University Law School Moot Court Competition. Prior to law school, she attended Miami University in Oxford, Ohio.

Chapter 5

James F. Bush is the principal shareholder of Bush Health Law PLLC and counsels clients throughout Florida and Washington in a variety of health law and litigation matters. Mr. Bush received his law degree from Stetson University and competed on its renowned Moot Court Board. After graduating, he served as outside litigation counsel to several of the largest long-term care providers in the United States. He founded his own practice in 2014 and now counsels individual and corporate clients in a variety of matters including provider malpractice, regulatory issues, and corporate affairs.

Chapter 6

Jacqueline Promislo is a member of Cozen O'Connor in its Philadelphia office. She focuses her practice on commercial litigation, product liability, insurance coverage, bad faith, employment discrimination, mass tort litigation, and breach of contract actions. Ms. Promislo is experienced in all phases of litigation, including extensive deposition experience, court appearances, bench and jury trials, arbitrations, mediations, witness preparation, and jury analysis. She double majored at McGill University and received her bachelor's in art history and political science. Ms. Promislo earned her law degree, cum laude, from Tulane University Law School.

Chapter 7

Janelle L. Davis is a trial lawyer and counselor who serves as the Assistant General Counsel to Thompson & Knight in Dallas, Texas, and is a partner in the firm's trial practice group. She focuses her practice on products liability, advertising, and general commercial litigation. She has experience in advising clients on how to mitigate litigation risk and managing mass tort cases including coordination with national and discovery counsel, expert witnesses, and trial counsel. She also has experience making and implementing strategic decisions throughout a case and drafting dispositive and *Daubert* motions. She has been recognized by Texas Rising Stars˙ by Thomson Reuters (2013–2015) and is an active member of the International Association of Defense Counsel. Ms. Davis received her JD, summa cum laude, from Pepperdine University School of Law and her BS, cum laude, from Texas Christian University.

John P. Atkins is counsel at Thompson Coburn LLP in Dallas, Texas. He received his law degree magna cum laude in May 2015 from the Dedman School of Law at Southern Methodist University, where he served as Associate Managing Editor for the *Journal of Air Law and Commerce*. While in law school, Mr. Atkins interned for the Honorable Michael Simon of the U.S. District Court for the District of Oregon and the Honorable Jorge Solis of the U.S. District Court for the Northern District of Texas. Mr. Atkins focuses his practice on general commercial litigation, health law, and insurance law. In his free time, Mr. Atkins coaches moot court.

Chapter 8

Kimberly Grant Silvus is a member of Wiseman Ashworth Law Group PLC, a boutique litigation firm in Nashville, Tennessee. Ms. Silvus entered private practice in 2007 and has concentrated her practice on defending physicians, hospitals, and long-term care facilities in healthcare liability actions. She represents healthcare providers before the state licensing boards in licensure and disciplinary matters, and she counsels healthcare providers in business and practice management matters. Ms. Silvus received her law degree from the University of Georgia School of Law, where she competed on the school's mock trial and moot court teams. She was a pupil in the Lumpkin Inn of Court and was named to the Order of the Barristers. After law school, she clerked for the Honorable Frank G. Clement Jr. of the Tennessee Court of Appeals. Ms. Silvus is a member of the Nashville Bar Association, the Tennessee Bar Association, and the American Bar Association and was selected to be a member of the TBA's Leadership Law Class of 2016. She is a past associate in the Harry Phillips American Inn of Court. She serves on the Board of Trustees for the Austin Peay Foundation and is the Chairperson of the Permanent Committee on Judiciary for the Cumberland Presbyterian Church. Ms. Silvus obtained a BA in foreign languages from Austin Peay State University and an MA in international boundaries from the University of Durham.

1

THE GENERAL COURSE OF MEDICAL MALPRACTICE LITIGATION

Nicole DeMaise, Leslie Isaacman Yohey, and Sarah Pazar Williams

This chapter is intended to introduce the general course of medical malpractice cases. Parties can face extensive and complex procedural requirements in the course of these lengthy, often unpredictable lawsuits. This chapter begins with a general fact scenario for a medical malpractice claim that will help frame the steps of a typical case. It goes on to address five distinct phases of medical malpractice litigation: (1) the initial investigation; (2) procedural considerations and the filing of suit; (3) pretrial discovery; (4) potential negotiations and settlement; and (5) preparing for and going to trial.

The first step in the course of a medical malpractice case is the initial investigation of the claim. A case should never be initiated without a thorough investigation of the circumstances surrounding the alleged harm. At the outset, the patient or the patient's family who is seeking to initiate the lawsuit should gather all relevant medical records. Upon gathering the records, when the patient or family meets with an attorney, the attorney should have a very detailed discussion with the patient or family about the facts of the case as well as any possible options for legal redress. The attorney should then investigate all potential defendants and consult with experts about standard of care and causation.

The second step involves various procedural hurdles and the filing of the actual lawsuit. This requires considerations about what legal issues and allegations are to be raised, relevant presuit notice requirements, applicable statutes of limitations, and party determinations, among other things.

The third step is pretrial discovery. Pretrial discovery involves written discovery in the form of interrogatories and requests for production. It also involves taking depositions of the parties and fact witnesses, including the patient and his relevant family members, as well as the caregivers who were involved in treating the patient. In addition, pretrial discovery involves retaining and disclosing experts who support the allegations or defenses, as well as deposing experts disclosed by other parties.

The fourth step involves negotiations and potential settlement. The overwhelming majority of medical malpractice cases settle out of court. Settlement negotiations can be informal between the lawyers for the parties, or they can occur in a formal process of mediation. Many times, these negotiations can cull issues for litigation and point out various strengths and weaknesses in the case.

The final step is preparing for and going to trial if the parties are unable to settle. The parties must prepare pretrial motions, opening statements, lay and expert witness testimony, exhibits to present in court, jury instructions, and closing arguments. The trial process can take many days or even weeks, and the outcome of trial will always be a calculated risk for all involved.

General Fact Scenario

The following fact scenario presents a very basic medical malpractice claim that will assist in outlining the general progression of a medical malpractice case:

> Peter Patient went to the hospital for a scheduled hip replacement surgery. After the surgery, he endured the postsurgical complication of infection at the surgical site. He was given penicillin for the infection. Peter unfortunately had an allergic reaction to the penicillin, which complicated his recovery and caused his hospital stay to be extended. He may face potential future complications as a result. Peter and his family approached Allison Attorney to discuss his options for filing suit against the hospital and the caregivers.

With this fact scenario in mind, we now look to the individual steps of litigating a medical malpractice case.

Initial Investigation

The first step in the course of a medical malpractice case is the initial investigation of the claim. When approached by a person such as Peter Patient, a plaintiff's lawyer such as Allison Attorney should engage in a thorough examination of the situation presented. More formal and robust discovery will be conducted once the lawsuit is filed, but having an understanding of the medical and legal issues before filing suit is imperative.

The medical records will ultimately be the best evidence of any medical malpractice claim. Typically, Peter should obtain a complete copy of his own medical records from the provider at issue (here, the hospital). He should also collect all records related to any care or treatment that is associated with the claim. For instance, if Peter followed up with his primary care physician regarding his allergic reaction in the hospital, those primary care physician records should be collected as well.

In general, it is easiest for a patient to obtain his own records from his healthcare providers. If anyone else, including the patient's attorney, requests the records, the requestor will need to provide an authorization that is compliant with the Health

Insurance Portability and Accountability Act of 1996 (HIPAA) and signed by the patient or the patient's representative.[1] In addition, while providers typically charge fees to copy and produce records for nonpatient requestors, many providers will waive fees for copying and producing records for the patient himself.[2]

After Peter has collected all relevant medical records, Allison should meet with Peter and discuss his situation and his potential lawsuit. The lawyer should conduct a thorough and detailed interview of the patient regarding his condition and treatment. She should get a comprehensive "story" from Peter that details exactly what happened and when, the injuries he suffered, who he believes is liable, and who (if anyone) he has spoken with about the situation. She should then talk with Peter about his options for legal redress as well as about what he ultimately hopes to gain from bringing a lawsuit. The attorney should retain a copy of the relevant medical records so that she can continue her investigation.

The attorney should then take the time to review the records herself. She should pay particular attention to specific dates of treatment, the names and charting of significant treating providers and caregivers, and any other details that might be germane to Peter's particular claims. The specific dates of treatment are relevant in considering applicable statutes of limitations. In addition, the names of providers are relevant to determine potential individually named defendants. The attorney should also look to the provider entity or entities, such as the hospital in Peter's situation, and perform a separate investigation of the entity or entities at issue. In addition to reviewing the records, the attorney may also want to consult medical literature that may be applicable to the claim at issue. During her investigation, the attorney should focus on two issues: first, was someone negligent in providing care or treatment? Second, if so, did any injury result from the negligent care or treatment?

With this initial information, the attorney must make a preliminary determination about whether she believes a medical malpractice case would be viable. If she determines that the case does not have merit, or if she is unwilling to represent the patient in a medical malpractice action, she should not hesitate to explain this to her client. In doing so, she should inform him that while she does not believe that his claims have merit, or while she is unwilling to represent him in this matter, another attorney might not feel the same way. She should also advise him of any relevant deadlines that may be approaching, particularly the running of the statute of limitations.

---

1. *See* 45 C.F.R. § 164.508.

2. HIPAA requires that healthcare providers furnish patients with copies of their medical records within 30 days of the request. In addition, under the Health Information Technology for Economic and Clinical Health Act (the HITECH Act), patients have the right to request their health information in electronic form. Generally, state law governs what providers can charge for supplying records, but providers are advised by the Department of Health and Human Services to charge no more than the actual supply and labor costs for responding to the request. *See* 45 C.F.R. § 164.524; 42 U.S.C. § 17935.

If, however, the attorney determines that Peter's medical malpractice case might be viable, she should retain one or more medical experts to review the medical records. Depending on various state law requirements, the expert should be actively practicing in the appropriate field of medicine that is relevant to the care at issue. The expert should review all of the medical records with a focus on the same issues: first, was someone negligent in providing care or treatment? Second, if so, did any injury result from the negligent care or treatment?

Knowing the expert's opinions, the attorney must then make a follow-up determination about the viability of a potential medical malpractice lawsuit. If the expert does not believe either that there was negligence or that said negligence caused any injury, the attorney should again not hesitate to explain this to her client, and she should terminate the representation. If, on the other hand, the expert believes that the case has merit, the attorney should, depending on applicable state law, obtain a signed written statement or affidavit from the expert establishing that, based on a review of the records, the claim has merit with respect to specified treating care providers. In accord with applicable state law, such a statement or affidavit may be required before filing suit.

Finally, before filing a lawsuit, the attorney should attempt to consult with the relevant providers involved in the care and treatment at issue.[3] In Peter's situation, this may include the surgeon, the physicians, and the nurses involved in his care. In addition, because his care involved a hospital entity, this may also include the hospital's claims or risk management professionals. The attorney should speak to these providers and claims or risk management professionals about what went wrong in the care and treatment of Peter and whether the situation can be remedied without filing suit. If remedy is not possible, Allison should go forward with making various procedural determinations and filing a lawsuit on Peter's behalf.

An initial investigation will necessarily take a different form from a defense perspective, as a defendant may not know about a claim until it has been filed or until presuit notice is provided. As soon as a provider finds out that a claim may be raised, the provider should take immediate action. At the outset, all relevant records, notes, and documentation that might be related to the claim should be located and preserved, and all potential responsible insurance carriers and claims or risk management professionals should be notified to alert them of the potential claim and to establish representation. The provider's attorney should, as soon as possible, obtain all relevant records from the provider, meet with the provider to get a full account of what happened, and perform a separate investigation on behalf of the provider. This may include interviews with the nurses and other staff members who provided care to the patient. When and if the provider is notified about the potential claim in advance of the lawsuit, there may also be specific time deadlines, established by state laws, to consider.

3. Consult applicable state rules regarding correspondence with medical providers or their employees, especially if attorneys are involved on the provider side.

Procedural Considerations and Filing Suit

Like any other lawsuit, a medical malpractice case is started with the filing of a complaint. There are a few special considerations that should be noted when preparing to file a medical malpractice complaint on behalf of a client.

Presuit Notice Requirements

Unlike regular negligence claims, before filing a complaint alleging medical malpractice, the attorney should first research whether the jurisdiction requires a presuit notice. Some jurisdictions statutorily require that written notice of potential claims be provided before suit is filed to each healthcare provider that will be a named defendant.[4] These statutory provisions usually set forth the information and level of detail that must be provided in the notice.[5] The notice requirement may also necessitate that a certain period of time pass before a complaint can be filed.[6] From the defendant's perspective, these notice requirements allow a defendant provider to investigate the potential claims, and potentially engage in settlement negotiations, before facing the time constraints associated with filing a formal answer.

Standard of Care Allegations

A medical malpractice complaint is generally filed in the same manner as any other negligence-based complaint, but special considerations do arise. Perhaps the most important thing that sets a medical malpractice complaint apart from a standard negligence claim is that a malpractice complaint must allege that a healthcare provider acted outside the standard of care. The standard of care is defined differently in each jurisdiction and is usually a community-based definition. It is generally defined as the degree of skill, learning, and experience ordinarily used, possessed, and practiced by such healthcare practitioners in the subject community or similar communities.[7]

Statute of Limitations and Statute of Repose

When filing the complaint, it is important to be aware of the jurisdiction's statute of limitations for medical malpractice cases and its effect, if any, on a client's claims. Each state will have its own statute of limitations for a medical malpractice

4. *See, e.g.*, TENN. CODE ANN. § 29-26-121.

5. *Id.*

6. This chapter does not discuss the implications of the waiting period on other claims that may be brought within the same action or the statute of limitations on those claims, which are issues that must be considered prior to filing suit.

7. *See, e.g.*, TENN. CODE ANN. § 29-26-101 *et seq.*

case, and the statute of limitations for medical malpractice actions functions in the same manner as other statutes of limitations.

It is important to be cognizant of not only the statute of limitations but also the statute of repose, if the jurisdiction has such a statute. Most states will have a statute of repose for a medical malpractice action.[8] This statute may be one or more years longer than the statute of limitations. The statute of repose bars any action that is commenced after the designated number of years following the alleged negligent act, regardless of when the injury is discovered.

A more complete discussion of statutes of limitations and statutes of repose is contained in Chapter 5.

Effects of Naming Certain Parties

The plaintiff must also consider which parties to join into the lawsuit. In some jurisdictions, there are statutory limitations placed on certain parties, which could impact a host of issues—from how much the plaintiff may recover, if successful, to whether a jury trial is permissible. For example, some jurisdictions place statutory limits on the amount of damages that may be recoverable from a governmental entity.[9] There may also be other restrictions on factors such as the availability of a jury trial.[10] Other jurisdictionally varying limitations may include caps on how much a plaintiff can recover for noneconomic tort damages.[11] Damages caps and other limitations are further discussed in Chapter 7.

Certificate of Good Faith or Affidavit of Merit

Before filing a complaint with the court, the attorney should also research whether the jurisdiction requires that a certificate of good faith, affidavit of merit, or other similar document be filed and served. While the content of these certificates or affidavits will vary according to jurisdiction, these documents are generally statements from an appropriately licensed or credentialed healthcare provider averring that she has reviewed the matter and believes that the healthcare provider defendant violated the standard of care.

Some jurisdictions require the affidavit to be filed contemporaneously with the complaint,[12] while others require that an affidavit be filed within a certain time subsequent to the filing of the complaint.[13] Failure to comply with these requirements, including their corresponding timeframes, may be fatal.

---

8. *See, e.g.*, TENN. CODE ANN. § 29-26-116.
9. *See, e.g.*, TENN. CODE ANN. § 29-20-101 *et seq.*
10. *Id.*
11. *See, e.g.*, TENN. CODE ANN. § 29-39-101 *et seq.*
12. *See, e.g.*, TENN. CODE ANN. § 29-26-122.
13. *See, e.g.*, N.J. STAT. ANN. § 2A:53A-22 *et seq.* (requiring an affidavit of merit be filed within 60 days of the first answer being filed, with a 60-day extension available).

Defendant's Pleading

From the defense perspective, after performing a thorough investigation and consulting with experts, the defendant files its responsive pleading. As with any other matter, this response may be in the form of a dispositive motion or an answer, or in some jurisdictions a combination of both. In jurisdictions where affidavits of similar healthcare providers are required, the defendant may also have the option to file a motion challenging the sufficiency of the affidavit prior to filing an answer.

Pretrial Discovery

After the lawsuit and responsive pleadings are filed and answered, the parties engage in pretrial discovery. Like any civil lawsuit, discovery in a medical malpractice case is conducted primarily through requests for production, interrogatories, and depositions. Expert discovery, however, is particularly important in medical malpractice actions.

Requests for Production: Medical Records and Other Documents

Before any formal discovery takes place, parties should ensure that they have complete copies of all relevant medical records. While much of this process may have been completed during the initial investigation, in order to maintain complete and accurate files and records, the parties' attorneys should not simply rely on documents provided by the other parties in response to requests for production. Instead, counsel should both request all relevant records in written discovery and request separate copies pursuant to authorization or subpoena. In addition, because the parties might be receiving multiple copies of records from multiple sources, it is advisable that they attempt to agree and commit to using sets of records that have consistent Bates labeling. This will help reduce confusion and allow unmistakable references to the records during the course of the litigation.

The necessary and relevant medical records might include records from third parties who are not involved in the lawsuit. For example, Peter Patient may have received treatment before or after his surgery from a physician or specialist who was not named as a defendant in the lawsuit regarding either his hip replacement surgery or his allergies. The defendants in Peter's lawsuit will want to obtain and review records from those providers to determine whether there were any other underlying issues with Peter's care and treatment, if Peter had other preexisting conditions that would not be readily apparent from the records relating to the surgery, or if Peter had complications subsequent to his surgery that may impact his damages.

In addition to requesting other relevant medical records, it may be necessary to make a separate request for supplementary documentation such as billing records or admission files depending on how these documents are named and how a particular facility organizes its documentation. Attorneys will also want to request records from any relevant pharmacies, clinics, home health agencies, ambulance services, laboratories, and other facilities or entities.

Medical records are subject to the rules and protections of HIPAA.[14] Any request for production of medical records or other personal health information must comply with the provisions of HIPAA to ensure patient privacy. This is true even when the patient is a plaintiff in a lawsuit that he himself initiated. Thus, even if Peter Patient may have informally "consented" to have his medical records released and reviewed by virtue of filing suit, counsel must still ensure either that Peter has signed proper medical authorizations permitting the release and review of his records or that subpoenas or document requests have been made through the court.[15]

Other relevant documents outside the scope of the medical records may include things such as phone records; facility policies and procedures; clinic schematics, diaries, or journals; handwritten notes; internal memos, e-mails, calendars, and calendar entries; text messages; and social media posts. All of these things should be specifically sought in requests for production. For example, with respect to social media posts, if Peter's sister posted on Facebook, three days after the cause of action accrued, "I can't believe that doctor gave Peter penicillin even though we told the nurse he was allergic," such information would be relevant and subject to discovery. Without robust document requests and a thorough investigation, that social media post, or other relevant detail, may go unnoticed.

Notably with respect to medical malpractice cases, many states have implemented statutory privileges to protect documents and information that were created as part of a medical peer review or quality assurance process or procedure. These so-called "investigational privileges" allow healthcare facilities to safely engage in quality assurance activities, such as fully investigating and documenting incidents and disciplinary matters, internally investigating the quality of care provided to patients, and providing education and training to personnel, without that information being used against the facility in a lawsuit. For instance, Peter's attorney may request the complete personnel files of Peter's nurses in written discovery; however, if a statutory peer review or quality assurance privilege applies, such discovery (or its scope) may be protected or limited. For a defendant, it is important to know about and preserve these privileges during the course of written discovery. The peer review, quality assurance, and other privileges will be discussed in more depth in Chapter 6.

Interrogatories

While the medical records provide essential information about the issues and claims in a medical malpractice lawsuit, rarely do they tell the whole story unaided. Accordingly, medical malpractice attorneys on both sides of a lawsuit use interrogatories to ascertain information and details about the theories, defenses, and applicable damages of the case. Typical medical malpractice interrogatories will

14. *See* 29 U.S.C. § 1181 *et seq.*

15. *See* 45 C.F.R. § 164.508.

request things such as (1) the identity of and information about caregivers, family members, or other fact witnesses; (2) information about conversations or documentation that may exist outside the medical record; (3) information about insurance, payment for services or medical equipment, and other issues relating to damages; (4) more detailed explanations about the treatments provided or withheld; (5) information about potential lay witnesses and their knowledge of the facts and circumstances at issue; (6) information about the professional background and experience of expert witnesses, as well as their expert opinions and the bases thereof; and (7) information about the parties' past lawsuits, including bankruptcies, criminal convictions, and other civil lawsuits, including any other medical malpractice claims.

It is also important to determine whether the party answering the interrogatories consulted with anyone other than counsel, such as a colleague or family member, in responding to the discovery requests. For instance, Peter Patient may have discussed his recollections of his hospitalization with his mother, who visited him in the hospital, while he was preparing the responses, or Peter's surgeon may have asked a colleague to assist him in responding to the interrogatories. The identity of these people can be sought through interrogatories; once known, the attorneys may wish to depose these people to determine what other information or insight they may have.

In addition to factual interrogatories, some attorneys will use so-called "contention" interrogatories, which directly inquire whether a party intends to rely on a certain fact or theory. Contention interrogatories help parties determine the other side's theory of the case and help taper the scope of the issues at the early stages of litigation. While contention interrogatories are not per se objectionable under the Federal Rules of Civil Procedure[16] or some state rules of civil procedure, courts may in their discretion defer parties' responses to contention interrogatories until later stages of discovery. This deferral may serve judicial economy in allowing broader, more substantial discovery to be conducted first.[17]

Medical Experts

Almost all medical malpractice cases will require testimony from a medical expert. Indeed, many states require expert testimony in all medical malpractice cases. Therefore, choosing the right medical expert is an essential step for both plaintiffs and defendants as early as possible in a lawsuit. Medical experts are so vital that

16. *See* FED. R. CIV. P. 33(a)(2) ("An interrogatory is not objectionable merely because it asks for an opinion or contention that relates to fact or the application of law to fact, but the court may order that the interrogatory need not be answered until designated discovery is complete, or until a pretrial conference or some other time.").

17. *See* Fisher & Porter Co. v. Tolson, 143 F.R.D. 93, 95 (E.D. Pa. 1992) (quoting Nestle Foods Corp. v. Aetna Cas. & Sur. Co., 135 F.R.D. 101, 110–11 (D.N.J. 1990)); *see also In re* Convergent Tech. Sec. Litig., 108 F.R.D. 328, 336 (N.D. Cal. 1985).

they receive their own chapter in this book (Chapter 8), but they are discussed here in broad strokes.

Medical experts provide opinions about the two most important questions in every medical malpractice case. First, was a healthcare provider negligent in providing care and treatment (i.e., did the healthcare provider follow the appropriate standard of care in treating this patient)? Second, if the standard of care was breached, did any injury result from the negligent care or treatment (i.e., did the failure to follow the appropriate standard of care cause injury to the patient)? An expert may testify about one or the other of these questions or both, depending on the case, her expertise, the requirements for expert testimony in that particular jurisdiction, and the strategic decisions of the attorney. Notably, some states stipulate that only physicians, rather than nurses or other treating care providers, can give expert opinions about causation. In addition, the circumstances of some cases may require that specialists in a particular field, rather than persons with general medical backgrounds, testify as experts. Therefore, before committing to the use of any specific experts, an attorney must first determine what kinds of experts, generally, she needs to retain to address these two questions.

For example, in Peter Patient's case, if allegations are raised against a physician for prescribing an incorrect medication as well as against the nursing staff for failing to catch the medication error, the attorneys must retain both a nursing expert to testify regarding the nursing standard of care and a physician expert to testify regarding *both* the medical standard of care *and* whether Peter was injured as a result of the alleged negligence. In addition, the attorneys may also want to retain a hospitalist physician expert to discuss the general practice of postsurgical treatment, as well as a pharmacologist to discuss the specific medications prescribed to Peter and their effects and complications given Peter's medical background and course of treatment. These decisions depend on the claims and defenses raised in the lawsuit, the statutory requirements for the jurisdiction, and the advisability and practicality of hiring multiple experts.

State rules of procedure and evidence vary as to who may testify as a medical expert. A person may qualify as a medical expert because of her academic achievements, her practical or clinical experience, her board certification, or any combination thereof. An attorney should rigorously investigate and research any potential experts she is considering to retain as a testifying medical expert. In addition to the objective qualifications, such as years of practice and educational information that can be found on an expert's curriculum vitae, an attorney should also ensure that the expert will be able to convey her opinion to the jury in an effective way. An expert should be able to instruct and assist the jury in navigating complex medical issues and to express her opinion in an understandable and persuasive manner. This difficult-to-define ability can be assessed by speaking extensively with the expert and by reviewing any testimony she has provided in other cases. In addition, the expert's previous testimony should be reviewed to discover prior opinions that might conflict with her testimony in the present matter.

An attorney should research and review the curriculum vitae and available prior testimony (both depositions and trial transcripts) of all disclosed experts to establish any grounds for objections as well as to ascertain any potential biases or weaknesses. For instance, a disclosed expert physician may have a long and extensive history of testifying as a defense expert, with no experience testifying on behalf of plaintiffs; as a result, an inference of bias in favor of providers may be raised. In another example, a disclosed expert physician may have authored a paper during her residency that contradicts a medical opinion to which she now plans to testify; because of this, there is a basis to contest or weaken her opinions. While issues such as these are not necessarily decisive for establishing biases or weaknesses in an expert's testimony, having information about the expert as early as possible is necessary both to avoid surprises and to raise relevant objections to the opposing party's experts throughout the course of litigation.

In addition to determining whether an expert has the proper expertise and whether she would successfully present her opinions to a jury, counsel should examine any jurisdiction-specific requirements regarding medical experts. Many states have a so-called "locality rule," which requires that an expert have practiced in that or an adjoining state and in the same community as or a similar community to the community at issue in a lawsuit. In addition, many states have statutes that require the expert to have practiced during a specific timeframe (e.g., one year) before or after the cause of action accrued. All of these issues should be considered very early on in the course of litigation so that time and money are not wasted and, more importantly, so that an otherwise qualified expert would not be barred from giving testimony after months of review and preparation.

An attorney should be very careful regarding what documents she presents to the expert and what she instructs the expert to do with respect to her own notes and files. In certain jurisdictions, the notes of an expert, which may include her draft opinions and disclosures, are discoverable. Attorneys should be aware of this and should instruct their retained expert witnesses to minimize their notetaking and written correspondence. Phone conversations are often the preferred method of communication with experts for this reason.

Finally, almost every jurisdiction requires written expert disclosures. These expert disclosures must contain a summary of the expert's opinions, the bases thereof, and a description of the expert's qualifications. Depending on the jurisdiction (and as required by the Federal Rules of Civil Procedure),[18] the expert disclosures may need to be prepared by the expert herself and may need to include a list of the expert's previous trial testimony. In efforts to afford the expert witness the benefit of reviewing all relevant information in advance of forming her opinions, the expert disclosures are typically the final step in written discovery.

---

18. *See* Fed. R. Civ. P. 26(a)(2)(B).

Depositions

After written discovery is complete, the parties will depose lay and expert witnesses. As with any civil lawsuit, this allows the attorneys to find out exactly what the witnesses know, to ascertain what they plan to testify about at trial, and to cross-examine them under oath.

Notably, medical malpractice cases often include a number of fact witnesses who might also be considered experts in their field; these are medical caregivers who treated the patient and thus have factual knowledge about the underlying litigation as well as medical expertise to opine regarding standard of care and causation. It is important to determine from the outset whether these witnesses will be testifying as fact witnesses, expert witnesses, or both and to make this designation clear on the record.

Preparing healthcare providers for deposition can present unique challenges. Most healthcare providers have been trained to instruct, explain, and assist the laypersons they are treating. This impulse can sometimes manifest in the deposition setting, which is a strict question-and-answer session rather than a conversation. Healthcare provider witnesses sometimes find themselves adding information and explanations beyond the scope of the questions or agreeing with broader statements than they intend because of this inclination to assist or help the attorney conducting the deposition. While this is of course a risk for all deponents, because healthcare providers are necessarily the "expert" in the room when it comes to medical issues, this risk is sometimes heightened. Deposition preparation can go a long way in refocusing a witness to the purpose of the deposition and to answering the questions presented.

Negotiations and Settlement

The conclusion of discovery and depositions often allows—and prompts—the parties to engage in meaningful settlement negotiations. Given the cost and uncertainty of litigation, medical malpractice cases often settle out of court. This settlement can be achieved through a formal mediation process or arbitration or through informal settlement discussions between the parties. When negotiating settlement of a medical malpractice case, there are a handful of factors to consider.

One primary area of concern for both parties is so-called "medical specials." Medical specials are a part of injury damages that are specifically provable through the bills associated with the claim. Medical bills alone can drive the cost of settlement up or down. Because medical malpractice cases involve alleged negligent medical treatment, the resultant damages are, at times, heftier than a non-medically-based personal injury matter, such as a slip and fall. Medical expenses are higher because they include both the costs of the underlying care as well as the costs of treating the patient's follow-up injuries and damages.

Both parties will want to check the law of collateral source or offsetting in their jurisdiction. It is important to remember that the application of collateral source or offsets may vary not only from jurisdiction to jurisdiction but also within jurisdictions as applicable to medical malpractice cases.

Medicare is a paramount consideration in all medical malpractice settlement negotiations, for all parties.[19] As with any other personal injury case, the parties will want to be fully aware of the existence and amount of a Medicare lien, if applicable. Medicare is entitled to reimbursement for all amounts paid toward medical treatment that resulted from the alleged negligence. Both parties will want to obtain a conditional payment letter from Medicare. It is important to ask Medicare to update this information throughout the course of the litigation so that the full amount of the Medicare lien is always known.

The amount of the Medicare lien can be especially problematic to the plaintiff (and conversely advantageous to the defense) when the Medicare lien is high and there is a cap on medical malpractice damages. Going back to Peter Patient, for example, assume that his jurisdiction has a \$1 million cap on medical malpractice tort damages and a \$250,000 cap on tort suits brought against governmental entities. Peter sues the hospital only, and the hospital is a public, governmental entity. As a result of the alleged negligence, Peter incurred \$300,000 in medical expenses due to his complicated hospital course. Medicare paid \$175,000 toward these medical expenses. Due to the tort caps in Peter's jurisdiction, the hospital's exposure is limited to \$250,000. The tort cap for governmental entities places quite a constraint on Peter's ability to recover damages, and this constraint must be acknowledged at the settlement table.

If settlement negotiations are successful and the parties enter into a settlement agreement, it is important for the defendant that the settlement agreement and release contain specific language addressing reimbursement of the Medicare lien.[20] Defense counsel will want to be particularly careful when dealing with Medicare, as defense counsel can be found liable to Medicare for failure to protect a Medicare lien.

Just as with Medicare, all parties will want to ascertain whether other liens are in place. These may include, but are by no means limited to, workers' compensation liens, state-funded insurance plan liens, and ERISA-based liens. To the extent that these liens exist, both parties will want to ensure that they are either satisfied or addressed in detail in the settlement release (to the extent allowable by law). The defendant will want to ensure that the settlement agreement and release contain an indemnification provision stating that plaintiff will indemnify the defendant, his agents, his attorneys, and all others for any lien that is unsatisfied by plaintiff.

19. This chapter does not go into the details, requirements, or nuances of Medicare, which are stringently regulated under federal law.

20. *See* 42 U.S.C. § 1395y(b)(7) (requiring submission of information by group health plans); *id.* § 1395y(b)(8) (requiring submission of information by liability insurers, including "self-insurers").

Trial Preparation and Trial

Medical malpractice cases are prepared and tried much like any other negligence case. While there are not many special considerations for medical malpractice cases, there are a few areas that may require additional focus.

All parties will want to make sure that they can authenticate the medical records and bills needed to support their case. One easy way to preauthenticate documents prior to trial is through the use of requests for admissions. Either party can serve such a request to ask the opposing party to admit that the document is authentic and kept in the regular course of business. Most parties will agree to the content of the medical records. When responding to requests for admissions about the authentication of medical records, it is important to ensure that the records at issue are a complete set before admitting that they are authentic. Notably, defense counsel should be cautious about the wording of any requests for admissions regarding the authentication of records, making sure that defense counsel does not admit, for example, that the medical bills are reasonable and necessary in the course of admitting the accuracy of the documents themselves.

Another major consideration for counsel in trying a medical malpractice case is the presentation and cross-examination of expert witnesses. Given the complexity of medicine and the limited knowledge of the laypersons on a jury, medical malpractice cases are generally expert driven. Prior to or at the beginning of trial, motions in limine can be filed by either party to limit the scope of an expert's testimony. In jurisdictions that require the service of written expert disclosure reports (such as federal court), a motion in limine can seek to limit the expert's testimony to the contents of those reports. In other jurisdictions that require only the filing of expert disclosures, counsel may want to serve amended and more detailed disclosures following the depositions of the opposing experts; in the event that the opposing party chooses not to depose an expert, this will prevent the opposing party from limiting the expert's testimony to the content of the written disclosure at trial.

Both parties will also want to work with their standard of care and causation experts to make sure each expert can communicate clearly and easily with the jury. If an expert cannot effectively convey her theories and opinions to a lay jury, her qualifications, education, experience, and opinions will not matter. Notably, the lawyers for both sides will also likewise want to ensure that, throughout the trial, they are explaining to the jury, in the simplest and clearest terms possible, what transpired and what damages, if any, resulted.

Finally, counsel for all parties will want to avoid getting lulled into an argument with the opposing expert witness during cross-examination. Even if there is great disdain for the witness, it is imperative to remain focused and ask only the necessary questions to support the case. It is best to know what can be expected from the witness and to leave it at that. The witness is, in fact, the expert, and she will know more than the lawyers. If a lawyer engages the expert in an argument on the stand, not only will the case lose focus, but the content-based argument likely will be lost as well.

Conclusion

In bringing or defending a healthcare liability lawsuit, attorneys should be aware of the particular nuances and facets of medical malpractice litigation. While they may be similar to general civil litigation cases in broad terms, medical malpractice cases are often subject to extensive and complex procedural requirements that are not part of general liability lawsuits. Thus, it is important to understand the general course of a medical malpractice case before taking on representation in such a case.

While this chapter is not intended to be a primer on the details of any specific area of medical malpractice litigation or the specific requirements of any jurisdiction, the information included in this chapter presents a working understanding of the general course of litigation in a medical malpractice case. The following chapters in this book provide greater detail about specific issues that may arise during the course of litigation.

2

COMMON ISSUES IN LONG-TERM CARE LITIGATION

Caldwell G. Collins and Brittany Bartley Simpson

Long-term care litigation involves an innately high-risk resident population with multiple preexisting comorbidities. Plaintiffs commonly allege more than one harm, and the operative residency can extend over months or even years, unlike a traditional one-event medical malpractice setting wherein, for example, a sponge is left in a surgical patient. Because of these unique challenges, the theme of this chapter is the highly fact-specific nature of long-term care litigation, which requires a specialized knowledge of the medical issues that arise in a medically fragile, often bed-bound, group.[1] It begins with a discussion of two threshold matters that often arise in long-term care litigation: arbitration agreements and the quality assurance privilege. It then moves to sources of liability, beginning with facility operations and ending with resident-specific considerations.

Arbitration Agreements

Alternative dispute resolution and arbitration agreements are common in the long-term care setting. Determining whether an enforceable arbitration agreement exists is an important step in the early litigation process, and disagreements over arbitrability can prove to be hearty battles.

The Federal Arbitration Act

The Federal Arbitration Act (FAA)[2] was enacted pursuant to the power of Congress to regulate commerce "to ensure judicial enforcement of privately made agreements to arbitrate."[3] Its purpose is to relieve congestion in the courts and to provide parties with an alternative method for dispute resolution that is speedier

1. This chapter does not contain an exhaustive list of issues that might arise in the long-term care context. For example, it does not cover Medicare fraud or worthless services cases under the False Claims Act.

2. 9 U.S.C. § 1 *et seq.*

3. Dean Witter Reynolds, Inc. v. Byrd, 470 U.S. 213, 219–20 (1985).

and less costly than litigation.[4] By enacting the FAA, Congress established a strong federal policy to support arbitration agreements, requiring that courts "rigorously enforce agreements to arbitrate."[5] Its passage represents Congress's effort to "reverse the long standing judicial hostility to arbitration agreements . . . and to place arbitration agreements upon the same foot as other contracts."[6]

Most states have also passed arbitration acts, many tracking the language of the FAA.[7] The language of a specific arbitration agreement may dictate whether the FAA applies to the agreement's enforcement and interpretation or whether state law applies. However, if the arbitration agreement is silent, there is an argument that the FAA applies, as long-term care facilities have myriad connections to interstate commerce (e.g., participation in federally funded Medicare and Medicaid programs, procurement of goods and supplies from other states, etc.), and therefore agreements related thereto may "involve interstate commerce" and fall within the bounds of the FAA.[8]

If a party files a complaint in arbitration or a motion to compel arbitration[9] and the opposition intends to contest the agreement, enforcement issues usually involve—depending on the specific jurisdiction—the scope of the arbitration agreement, the signatory's authority or capacity to enter into the arbitration agreement, the agreement's substantive conscionability, and the agreement's procedural conscionability.

Scope of the Arbitration Agreement

If a signed arbitration agreement exists, counsel must first determine whether the claim at issue is within the scope of that agreement. This requires a close reading of the language of the agreement itself. Is it limited to certain types of claims? Does it cover all claims that arise between a resident and a long-term care facility? Does it apply to the resident's multiple stays, or is it specifically limited to certain dates? Arbitration agreements that are phrased in terms of all claims or controversies relating in any way to the resident's stay(s) at the facility will typically cover medical malpractice claims of any kind. Before filing a motion to compel arbitration, counsel must ensure that she has a valid argument that the claims at issue fall within the agreement's terms.

---

4. *See* Allied-Bruce Terminix Cos. v. Dobson, 513 U.S. 265, 278 (1995); Gilmer v. Interstate/Johnson Lane Corp., 500 U.S. 20, 31 (1991); Southland Corp. v. Keating, 465 U.S. 1, 7 (1984).

5. Shearson/Am. Express, Inc. v. McMahon, 482 U.S. 220, 226 (1987) (citations omitted).

6. *Gilmer*, 500 U.S. at 24.

7. *See, e.g.*, LA. REV. STAT. ANN. § 9:4201 *et seq.*

8. *See, e.g.*, Owens v. Nat'l Healthcare Corp., 263 S.W.3d 876 (Tenn. 2008).

9. When moving to compel arbitration, parties may want to move for a stay of merits discovery pending resolution of the arbitration issue (which may itself require pointed discovery before a hearing).

Capacity and Authority

If a mentally competent nursing home resident signs his own arbitration agreement upon admission to a facility, authority is not an issue in enforcement of the arbitration agreement. The issue of whether the signatory properly signed typically arises if the resident's ability to contract is in question on the day the arbitration agreement was signed, or if someone other than the resident signed. If the resident signed for himself and has a history of mental incapacity, careful examination of the medical record is necessary. Because individuals are generally presumed competent to contract,[10] a finding of incompetency by a physician, or an expert opinion on the resident's mental state at the time of execution, may be required.

If someone other than the resident signed, state law regarding that individual's authority to contract for the resident will control.[11] The signatory's authority may be established by an executed written document, such as a general power of attorney, a power of attorney for healthcare, or a healthcare surrogate form;[12] through the act of a competent principal, such as express oral or written authority or implied authority; through judicial appointment, such as a conservatorship; or through a statutory scheme, such as a healthcare surrogate statute. Some of these authority avenues may not be available under a given state's law, so it is essential to understand the applicable law regarding circumstances under which different agents may act for long-term care residents and the scope of their powers.

Substantive Unconscionability

The substantive unconscionability inquiry examines whether the arbitration agreement terms are unclear or unreasonably favorable to one party, usually the party seeking enforcement. These disputes typically involve one or more of the following issues:

- Was the arbitration provision clearly defined, whether stand-alone or within an admissions agreement?
- Were the terms of the arbitration agreement plain or easy to understand?

---

10. *See, e.g.*, Rawlings v. John Hancock Mut. Life Ins. Co., 78 S.W.3d 291, 297 (Tenn. Ct. App. 2001).

11. The FAA provides that written arbitration agreements shall be enforceable "save upon such grounds as exist at law or in equity for the revocation of any contract." 9 U.S.C. § 2. A court's determination of the scope of an arbitration agreement is guided by "general state-law principles of contract interpretation," and "due regard must be given to the federal policy favoring arbitration." Volt Info. Sci., Inc. v. Bd. of Trustees, 489 U.S. 475, 475–76 (1989).

12. The particular arbitration agreement in conjunction with state law will also determine whether entrance into an arbitration agreement is a legal decision, a healthcare decision, or a hybrid of the two. This will affect who can sign for the resident. For example, if entrance into an arbitration agreement is a pure legal decision in the relevant jurisdiction, a healthcare surrogate form is unlikely to establish authority to enter into the arbitration agreement for the principal.

- Does the arbitration agreement state that the parties are giving up the right to a jury trial?
- Does the arbitration agreement specify what law or procedure applies?
- Does the arbitration agreement provide for selection of a neutral arbitrator?
- Does the arbitration provide for selection of a convenient venue?
- Does the arbitration agreement address when claims may be appealed?
- Does the arbitration agreement bind both parties?
- Does the arbitration agreement contain a revocation clause?
- Does the arbitration agreement affect the facility's duty to use reasonable care with regard to the resident?
- Is the arbitration agreement voluntary or mandatory?

At its core, the substantive unconscionability question is one of state law contract enforcement, so counsel should consult applicable law when evaluating the items above to determine if the black-and-white terms of the arbitration agreement are equitable.

Procedural Unconscionability

Procedural unconscionability refers to unfairness in the bargaining process itself. This concerns how and when the facility presented the arbitration agreement to the resident or his agent. When evaluating procedural unconscionability, consider factors such as the following:

- Could the signatory read?
  - Was the signatory given the opportunity to read the entire agreement or have it read to him?
  - Did the signatory decline the opportunity to read the agreement or have it read to him?
- Was the agreement in a language that the signatory could understand?
- If the arbitration agreement was explained, what was the substance of the explanation?
- If the facility representative provided an explanation, did she misrepresent any terms of the arbitration agreement?
- Did the signatory ask questions?
- Did the signatory voice any clear or obvious misunderstanding about the material terms of the arbitration agreement?
- Was the signatory offered a copy of the arbitration agreement?

Procedural unconscionability is an intensely fact-specific inquiry that incorporates issues such as the sophistication of the signatories and their behavior during execution. Counsel must consider all of the circumstances surrounding execution of the arbitration agreement when arguing for or against its enforcement.

CMS Regulation of Long-Term Care Arbitration Agreements

On October 4, 2016, the Centers for Medicare & Medicaid Services (CMS) published a final rule banning predispute arbitration agreements in the long-term care setting. The American Health Care Association and a group of affiliated nursing homes challenged the rule in the U.S. District Court for the Northern District of Mississippi, and the court preliminarily enjoined enforcement of the regulation.[13] In 2017, CMS issued proposed revisions to the 2016 rule and took public comments. Then, on July 16, 2019, CMS issued a revised final rule advising that binding arbitration agreements *are* permissible in long-term care facilities that receive federal funding and imposing certain requirements on them.[14] While the 2019 final rule may be challenged in court, as of the date of publication, federal regulations require the following of long-term care arbitration agreements:

- the arbitration agreement must not be a condition of admission or continued care, it must explicitly state that it is not mandatory, and the facility must explicitly inform the resident or his representative that it is not mandatory;
- the agreement must be explained in a manner that the signatory understands, including in a language the signatory understands;
- the signatory must acknowledge that he understands the agreement;
- the agreement must provide for the selection of a neutral arbitrator to which both parties agree;
- the agreement must provide for selection of a venue that is convenient to both parties;
- the agreement must allow revocation within 30 calendar days of execution; and
- the agreement may not contain any language prohibiting or discouraging communication with federal, state, or local officials.

The final rule also requires that long-term care facilities retain copies of signed arbitration agreements for five years following resolution of a dispute through arbitration.[15]

While the 2019 final rule provides a road map for enforcement of arbitration agreements, it is important to note that federal and state substantive law still apply.

Quality Assurance

The quality assurance/performance improvement (commonly referred to as QAPI) process is integral to long-term care facility operations. Facility QAPI

13. Am. Health Care Ass'n v. Burwell, 217 F. Supp. 3d 921 (N.D. Miss. 2016).
14. 84 Fed. Reg. 34718-01; *see* 42 C.F.R. 483.70(n).
15. 42 C.F.R. 483.70(n).

committees assist in tracking and trending issues in the care provided and improving quality of care where needed. Attorneys representing residents may argue that quality assurance materials should be discoverable, as they may contain medical information pertaining to the subject resident. Attorneys defending facilities will argue to shield those materials and will contend that any records relevant to the resident are part of the chart and that the quality assurance records are used for the larger purpose of assessing overall quality of care in the facility and are therefore protected by the state or federal quality assurance privilege.[16] While the details of this privilege are addressed in Chapter 6, attorneys litigating long-term care cases must understand the types of documents that are commonly the subject of quality assurance discovery battles. Examples of these documents include

- incident/accident reports;
- incident/accident investigation notes;
- incident/accident follow-up measures;
- staff interviews or statements regarding incidents or investigations;
- staff performance evaluations;
- staff disciplinary or corrective actions;
- tracking and trending reports, such as skin integrity reports, fall incident reports, and infection rate reports;
- documents evaluating reasonableness of healthcare costs;
- minutes of a quality assurance, quality improvement, or peer review committee; and
- documents generated by or for a quality assurance, quality improvement, or peer review committee.

Generally, quality assurance documents are those geared toward assessment of the facility's performance for overall improvement of care at the facility, as opposed to specific care information, diagnoses, or treatments with regard to a particular resident (i.e., information that should be in the resident's chart). When determining which documents should be protected and which should be discoverable, counsel should consult the pertinent statutes and the law interpreting them.

Facility Operations as a Source of Liability

CMS Surveys

State governments oversee the licensing of nursing homes and contract with CMS to monitor facilities that want to be eligible to provide care to Medicare and Medicaid patients. CMS works with individual states to conduct surveys of nursing homes to determine compliance with federal regulations. These surveys evaluate facility performance on every level, from resident care to staff interaction to facility administration. Surveyors also inspect the medical records of specific residents.

16. *See, e.g.,* 42 U.S.C. § 11111; Tenn. Code Ann. § 68-11-272; Miss. Code Ann. §§ 41-63-9, 41-63-23; Ala. Code Ann. § 21-22-8; La. Rev. Stat. § 13:3715.3.

There are multiple types of surveys, but annual surveys (which occur approximately every 12 months or more frequently in the case of poor performance) and complaint surveys are the most common. Lasting anywhere from a few days to over a week, annual surveys seek to evaluate the overall level of care provided and identify ongoing problems within the facility. Complaint surveys occur in response to a specific complaint or incident at the facility, whether reported by the facility itself or by a concerned citizen.

While the survey process itself is outside the scope of this chapter, issues involving survey results and history can arise in a long-term care case. For lawyers that represent the plaintiff, depending on the issues in the lawsuit, a bad survey result can support their position. For lawyers that represent the facility, a good survey result can bolster an argument that there was no breach of the standard of care with regard to a particular resident at issue. Therefore, it is advisable to research the facility's survey history at the case's inception and important to determine whether the particular resident was a subject of the survey. Each survey assessing resident care samples resident charts, and the sample residents' names appear on a survey "key." The earlier attorneys uncover that information, the more likely they are able to effectively use or defend against the survey.

Staffing

Federal and state regulations require that nursing homes be staffed at certain minimum levels.[17] Staffing refers to the number and quality of nurses and Certified Nursing Assistants (CNAs), who provide assistance with daily, routine care in nursing homes. Lack of staffing or improperly trained staff is a theme that appears in many long-term care cases.

If an allegation of low staffing arises regarding the day (or period) in question, attorneys litigating the suit must look further into the details of the inadequate staffing. How far was the staffing below federal or state minimum standards? Did the low staffing impact the quality of care? Was the staff member in question adequately trained? If poor staffing is proven, the inquiry then moves to causation: was the lack of staff the cause of the resident's condition? Or was it unavoidable, given the resident's medical history and course of treatment? Conversely, if a facility is staffed in compliance with state and federal regulations, or has staff that is well trained, these facts can be a boon to the defense.

Budgeting

In recent years, long-term care plaintiffs have attempted to point to facility budgets as a source of liability. For example, in *Hernandez v. Golden Gate Equity Holdings, LLC*,[18] a class action filed in San Francisco Superior Court, the plaintiffs claimed

---

17. *See, e.g.*, Tenn. Comp. R. & Regs. 1200-08-06-.06 (requiring two hours of direct care to each resident every day, including 0.4 hours of licensed nursing personnel time); 42 C.F.R. § 483.30.

18. Case No. CGC 10-505288 (S.F., Cal. Super. Ct.) (filed Nov. 10, 2010).

that the defendant facility conspired to increase its profits through a "pervasive and intentional failure"[19] to provide the minimum number of skilled nursing hours under applicable California law. While the class action context is at the far end of the spectrum, the issue also arises in single-plaintiff cases. Plaintiffs typically argue that the facility is drastically or intentionally underfunded in a way that affects residents, and facilities maintain that budgetary information has no bearing on the care rendered to the individual patient. This reinforces the recurring theme of this chapter: each inquiry is highly fact specific.

Specific Resident Care as a Source of Liability

Standard of Care for Nursing Facilities

It is a general rule of law that a nursing facility should exercise reasonable care to avoid physical injury and mental distress to its residents, and the reasonableness of such care is to be assessed and measured in light of the resident's physical and mental incapacitations.[20] Nevertheless, a nursing facility is not an insurer of its residents and is not required to provide a nurse or attendant to monitor a resident 24 hours a day.[21] The applicable standard of care is determined by state law and takes into account the locality of the facility in question and the circumstances specific to the resident. In most circumstances, the standard of care must be established by expert testimony.

The Nursing Home Reform Act

In response to reports of widespread neglect and abuse in nursing homes, Congress enacted legislation in 1987 known as the Nursing Home Reform Act, which mandates compliance from all skilled nursing facilities receiving Medicare or Medicaid funds. The objective of the act is to set minimum regulatory requirements for the industry and provide standards for assessing a resident, documenting care, and maintaining dignity and respect.[22] However, some states have adopted more stringent laws. In addition to covering skilled nursing facilities, many states have adopted parts of the Nursing Home Reform Act to govern minimum standards for assisted living facilities.

19. *Id.*, Compl. at 2 ¶ 1.
20. Juhnke v. Evangelical Lutheran Good Samaritan Soc., 634 P.2d 1132, 1136 (Kan. Ct. App. 1981).
21. Murphy v. Allstate Ins. Co., 295 So. 2d 29, 34 (La. Ct. App. 1974) (citing LeBlanc v. Midland Nat'l Ins. Co., 219 So. 2d 251 (La. App. 1969)).
22. 42 C.F.R. § 483.1(b).

Residents' Rights

Under federal law, residents of long-term care facilities are guaranteed certain rights. 42 U.S.C. § 1395i-3 makes facilities responsible for the protection and promotion of these rights, which include

- **Free choice:** The right to choose a personal attending physician, to be fully informed in advance about care and treatment, to be fully informed in advance of any changes in care or treatment that may affect the resident's well-being, and (except with respect to a resident adjudged incompetent) to participate in planning care and treatment or changes in care and treatment.
- **Freedom from restraints:** The right to be free from physical or mental abuse, corporal punishment, involuntary seclusion, and any physical or chemical restraints imposed for purposes of discipline or convenience and not required to treat the resident's medical symptoms. Restraints may only be imposed—
  - to ensure the physical safety of the resident or other residents, and
  - only upon the written order of a physician that specifies the duration and circumstances under which the restraints are to be used (except in emergency circumstances specified by the Secretary until such an order could reasonably be obtained).
- **Privacy:** The right to privacy with regard to accommodations, medical treatment, written and telephonic communications, visits, and meetings of family and of resident groups.
- **Confidentiality:** The right to confidentiality of personal and clinical records and to access current clinical records of the resident upon request by the resident or the resident's legal representative, within 24 hours (excluding hours occurring during a weekend or holiday) after making such a request.
- **Accommodation of needs:** The right—
  - to reside and receive services with reasonable accommodation of individual needs and preferences, except where the health or safety of the individual or other residents would be endangered, and
  - to receive notice before the room or roommate of the resident in the facility is changed.
- **Grievances:** The right to voice grievances with respect to treatment or care that is (or fails to be) furnished, without discrimination or reprisal for voicing the grievances, and the right to prompt efforts by the facility to resolve grievances the resident may have, including those with respect to the behavior of other residents.
- **Participation in resident and family groups:** The right of the resident to organize and participate in resident groups in the facility and the right of the resident's family to meet in the facility with the families of other residents in the facility.

- **Participation in other activities:** The right of the resident to participate in social, religious, and community activities that do not interfere with the rights of other residents in the facility.
- **Examination of survey results:** The right to examine, upon reasonable request, the results of the most recent survey and any plan of correction in effect with respect to the facility.
- **Refusal of certain transfers:** The right to refuse a transfer to another room within the facility, if a purpose of the transfer is to relocate the resident from a portion of the facility that is a skilled nursing facility to a portion of the facility that is not such a skilled nursing facility.[23]

Attorneys litigating long-term care cases should be aware of these, and any state-imposed, residents' rights when assessing the care provided by the facility. Commitment to honoring residents' rights or the converse—systematic violation of those rights—can impact the value of a case.

Policy and Procedure Manuals

Every long-term care facility will maintain a set of written policies and procedures that establish guidelines for the facility's various processes and care. Some are required by law,[24] and others are unique to the particular facility. Policies and procedures can govern everything from the admission process to medication administration to emergency response. While they do not set the standard of care, policies and procedures can be a window into facility operations.

Because policies and procedures vary greatly in their content and specificity, it is crucial for attorneys litigating a long-term care case to analyze the specific policies and procedures applicable to the facility at issue to determine whether they affect the suit. For example, a policy *requiring* that a resident be transferred in a certain manner in every circumstance might present an issue in litigation if the resident was transferred in another way and fell as a result. Attorneys must then consider the policy in conjunction with the surrounding facts and the resident's conditions. What were the circumstances surrounding the transfer? Did a doctor or nurse recommend a different type of transfer given the resident's needs in that precise circumstance? What did the resident's care plan provide? In such a case, the facility's policy and procedure manual may begin the inquiry but cannot be considered in a vacuum.

Note that policy and procedure manuals may be proprietary in nature; a proper protective order should be in place before they are produced.

---

23. 42 U.S.C. § 1395i-3(c)(1)(A). The foregoing list includes specified rights but is not an all-inclusive list of residents' rights. Consult the full text of 42 U.S.C. § 1395i-3 for a complete list of residents' rights.

24. *See, e.g.*, 42 U.S.C. § 1395cc(f)(1) (requiring written policies and procedures regarding advance directives).

The Medical Record

A resident's medical record is the first item reviewed by plaintiff's counsel to determine whether a facility has met the standard of care in treatment of a resident. It is also the first line of defense for a facility and nursing staff. Depending on the level of care (skilled nursing, assisted living, etc.), the medical record may include advance directives; admission assessments and follow-up assessments; care plans; physician orders; progress notes; nurse's notes; medication and treatment records; rehabilitation therapy notes and logs; social services/activities records; behavioral notes; records of activities of daily living; and nutritional services notes. Skilled nursing facilities and nursing facilities will have more robust charting—many assisted living facilities, for example, chart on residents only by exception (i.e., when something out of the ordinary happens).

The Nursing Home Reform Act sets forth requirements for long-term care facilities regarding assessment of a resident upon admission, development of an appropriate care plan for a resident, and maintenance of accurate and complete clinical records.[25]

Assessing a Resident's Needs and Creating a Plan of Care

The Nursing Home Reform Act requires a facility to make a comprehensive assessment of a resident's needs within 14 days after admission and within 14 days after the facility determines there has been a significant change in the resident's physical or mental condition.[26] The facility must develop a care plan for each resident that includes measurable objectives and timetables to meet the medical, nursing, and mental needs identified in the assessment.[27] This care plan must be developed within seven days after completion of a comprehensive assessment.[28] Care plans can include measures to prevent pressure sores, infections, falls, significant weight loss, dehydration, etc.

When reviewing a medical chart to assess potential liability, attorneys litigating long-term care cases should look for resident assessments, implementation of care plans depending on length of residency, and updates to care plans, if indicated.

Documentation Errors

Any lawyer familiar with healthcare litigation knows that no medical chart is perfect, but egregious documentation errors—especially documentation that fails to meet federal and state minimum charting requirements—can form the basis of liability. Counsel and their experts should review the medical record for documentation errors, examples of which include (1) material inconsistencies

25. *See* 42 C.F.R. § 483.20; 42 C.F.R. § 483.75.
26. *Id.* § 483.20(b).
27. *Id.* § 483.20(k).
28. *Id.*

in documentation among the facility's staff; (2) failure to document significant events (e.g., falls, pressure sores); (3) fraudulent documentation (e.g., wrongfully changing or backdating entries); and (4) impossibility in documentation (e.g., charting when the staff member is not at work or charting when the resident is at the hospital).

Specific Care Issues

The Nursing Home Reform Act provides that skilled nursing facilities should "provide services and activities to attain or maintain the highest practicable physical, mental, and psychosocial well-being of each resident in accordance with a written plan of care."[29] While most long-term healthcare facilities provide competent and comprehensive care to their residents, there are instances when the quality of care does not meet the standard of care for a resident's needs. This gives rise to claims of malpractice, abuse, or neglect. Some of the more common signs of resident abuse or negligence include, but are not limited to, injuries requiring emergency treatment or hospitalization; heavy medication or sedation; rapid, unexplained weight loss; egregious lack of personal hygiene; and open wounds, cuts, bruises, or welts.

While there are myriad resident-specific care issues that form the basis of long-term care cases, the most cited claims of negligence or malpractice against a nursing facility include a resident developing pressure sores, a resident being injured due to a fall, a resident becoming dehydrated or developing a urinary tract infection, the inappropriate use of restraints on a resident, and egregious medication errors.

Pressure Sores

In clinical terms, pressure sores may be referred to as decubitus ulcers, pressure ulcers, or bed sores. Pressure sores are a common condition found in many residents of nursing homes. Although they are quality indicators under the Medicare/Medicaid guidelines, there is still academic debate and controversy about whether pressure sores, generally, are preventable, especially in a population prone to natural skin breakdown.

The Nursing Home Reform Act requires a facility to assess a resident's current skin condition upon admission and implement an appropriate plan of care.[30] Disregarding risk factors and failing to create an appropriate plan of care can expose a facility to liability. For example, in *Livingston Care Center v. U.S. Department of Health & Human Services*, when a skilled nursing facility appealed federal fines for deficiencies related to patient pressure sores, the United States Court of Appeals for the Sixth Circuit strongly considered the individual patients' physical

29. *Id.* § 483.25.
30. *Id.* § 483.20.

conditions.[31] The court discussed each resident's comorbidities, highlighted the specific pressure sore risk factors that applied, and pointed to details in the record that revealed that the facility did not use appropriate pressure-relieving devices or procedures.[32] The court found that the nonuse of those devices constituted noncompliance under federal law.[33] These undisputed facts, along with other substandard care factors, led the court to uphold the deficiency fines against the facility.[34]

Plaintiff's counsel may request compensatory damages, pain and suffering, loss of enjoyment of life, and even third-party damages for mental distress in claims of negligence relating to pressure sores. Extreme cases of pressure sore negligence may lead to punitive damages. In one such example, a 76-year-old nursing home resident developed 16 pressure sores that, when left untreated, progressed to the resident's bone.[35] The plaintiff presented evidence that these pressure sores, in conjunction with malnourishment and dehydration, led to the resident's death. The jury awarded $2.8 million in compensatory damages and $310 million in punitive damages based on the facility's negligence.

When evaluating a chart for pressure sore liability, counsel and their experts should consider evidence of pressure sore risk factors, pressure sores in existence upon admission, pressure sore development or worsening, pressure sore treatment and interventions, and use of pressure-relieving devices.

Falls

Falls are a constant risk for the elderly and remain one of the more difficult types of incidents to prevent in the long-term care setting. Because of their underlying comorbidities, nursing home residents generally suffer from fall risk factors at a higher rate than others living in the community. In fact, various studies indicate that as many as 50 to 75 percent of nursing home residents in the United States fall at least once a year, with many residents falling more than once.[36] And because federal policy provides that residents are to be afforded the least restrictive environment possible (i.e., with either no or minimal restraints), falls are often inevitable.[37]

Because they are so common, falls are frequently at the center of long-term care litigation. For example, in *Russell v. Kossover*, a jury found for the plaintiff and awarded $46,600 in damages where a nursing home resident with a history of falls

31. Livingston Care Ctr. v. U.S. Dep't of Health & Human Servs., 388 F.3d 168 (6th Cir. 2004).

32. Risk factors discussed included peripheral vascular disease, incontinence, dependence on staff for daily activities, and other notations on the plan of care. *Id.* at 173.

33. "[F]ailure to provide the requisite pressure relieving devices listed in his plan of care constitutes a sufficient basis for a finding of noncompliance under 42 C.F.R. § 483.25(c)." *Id.*

34. *Id.* at 176.

35. Fuqua v. Horizon/CMS Healthcare Corp., No. 4:9800-CV-1087-Y, 2001 WL 267650 (N.D. Tex. Feb. 14, 2001).

36. Laurence Z. Rubenstein et al., *The Value of Assessing Falls in an Elderly Population*, 113(4) Annals of Internal Med. 308, 316 (1990).

37. 42 U.S.C. § 1395(i)-3(c)(1)(A)(ii).

was discovered on the floor of her room with a broken hip.[38] In *Gaddis v. Chatsworth Health Care Center, Inc.*, the court found that relatives of a nursing home resident failed to establish negligence against the nursing home as a result of the resident's falls.[39] When defending these cases, counsel and their experts should consider issues such as preexisting fall risks (including weakness, gait problems, previous falls, medications, etc.), fall risk assessments, implementation of care plans and fall prevention interventions, primary care provider recommendations, and federal/state/local environmental requirements for grab bars and other mobility-assisting measures.[40]

Dehydration/Urinary Tract Infections

Dehydration in nursing homes is prevalent due to a number of factors. Some common medications for high blood pressure and depression have diuretic properties or cause elevated levels of perspiration. Additionally, the sense of thirst becomes less acute with age, and some nursing home residents are unable to obtain fluids independently. Urinary tract infections (UTIs) are the most common and frequent bacterial infection found in long-term care facility residents, with surveys across different facilities indicating that 15 to 30 percent of men and 25 to 50 percent of women have positive urine cultures.[41] Due to the closely related medical treatment and care issues between dehydration and UTIs, these topics will be discussed together in this section.

The Nursing Home Reform Act states that a facility must provide "sufficient fluid intake to maintain proper hydration and health."[42] It also addresses UTIs, providing that facilities should ensure residents are catheterized only when necessary and that those residents who are catheterized "receive appropriate treatment and services to prevent" UTIs.[43]

The presence of dehydration and UTIs can create serious liability for nursing homes. In *Frieh v. Life Care Centers of America Inc.*, an Arizona jury returned a $1.5 million verdict for an 81-year-old nursing home resident who developed dehydration and a urinary tract infection that resulted in sepsis, among other alleged injuries.[44] In *Manor Care, Inc., et al. v. Douglas*, an 87-year-old female resident suffering from Alzheimer's dementia, Parkinson's disease, and other health issues was admitted to a nursing home facility. She was able to communicate and was well hydrated upon entering the facility. Over the course of 19 days, the resident

38. Russell v. Kossover, 634 So. 2d 72 (La. Ct. App. 1994).

39. Gaddis v. Chatsworth Health Care Ctr., Inc., 282 Ga. App. 615 (Ct. App. 2006).

40. *See* Wayne A. Ray et al., *A Randomized Trial of Consultation Service to Reduce Falls in Nursing Homes*, 278 JAMA 557–62 (1997).

41. Lindsay E. Nicolle & Thomas T. Yoshikawa, *Urinary Tract Infection in Long-Term Care Facility Residents*, 31 Clinical Infectious Diseases 757 (2000).

42. 42 C.F.R. § 483.25(j).

43. *Id.* § 483.25(d).

44. Frieh v. Life Care Ctrs. of Am. Inc., No. CV2003-023180, 2006 WL 4543746 (Ariz. 2006).

became severely dehydrated, developed other health issues, and died as a result of severe dehydration. The estate sued the nursing home and won a jury trial verdict of $11.5 million in compensatory damages and $80 million in punitive damages. Ultimately, the Supreme Court of Appeals of West Virginia upheld the availability of punitive damages but exercised a remittitur that reduced the punitive damages amount to $32 million.[45]

When allegations of potential dehydration or UTIs arise, counsel and their experts should look into the resident's history of infection, care planning and interventions to address fluid intake and infection prevention, intake and output records if available, medication administration, infection control measures, and response to positive infection tests.

Restraints

The Nursing Home Reform Act explicitly states that residents' rights include the right generally to be free from "physical or chemical restraints."[46] Restraints may be allowed if both the restraint ensures the physical safety of the restrained resident or other residents,[47] and the restraint is administered upon the written order of a physician that specifies the duration and circumstances of use.[48] The exception to the two-part restraint requirement under the act is for emergency circumstances as specified by the Secretary of Health and Human Services.[49] This restriction on restraints has been championed as one of the leading features of the entire Nursing Home Reform Act and is credited with a significant increase in the overall quality of residents' lives.[50]

A physical restraint is defined as "any manual method or physical or mechanical device, material, or equipment attached or adjacent to the resident's body that the individual cannot remove easily which restricts freedom of movement or normal access to one's body."[51] The most common application of physical restraints is for residents who suffer from dementia and related illnesses that cause wandering-type behavior that puts them at a greater risk for falls and other physical harm. A chemical restraint is defined as a psychopharmacologic drug used for discipline or convenience rather than the treatment of medical symptoms.[52] The primary distinction for chemical restraints is the purpose for which the drug is administered: if the purpose is to make a job easier for the caretaker or nursing home, then it is a restraint; but if the drug is administered in accordance with a medical need, then it is not a chemical restraint.

45. Manor Care, Inc., et al. v. Douglas, 763 S.E.2d 73 (W. Va. 2014).

46. 42 U.S.C. § 1395i-3(c)(1)(A)(ii); *see also* Residents' Rights section, *supra*.

47. 42 U.S.C. § 1395i-3(c)(1)(A)(ii)(I).

48. *Id.* § 1395i-3(c)(1)(A)(ii)(II).

49. *Id.*

50. Norman G. Castle et al., *Physical Restraints in Nursing Homes: A Review of the Literature Since the Nursing Home Reform Act of 1987*, 55 Med. Care Res. Rev. 171 (June 1998).

51. Interpretive Guidance to 42 U.S.C. § 1395i-3(c)(1)(A)(ii).

52. *Id.*

Liability for the improper use of restraints can take many forms, including medical negligence, wrongful death, statutory violations, improper prescription of psychotropic medications, physical injury, and impairment of mental or physical function. For example, in *Estate of Hendrickson ex rel. Hendrickson v. Genesis Health Venture, Inc.*, the plaintiff alleged liability arising from the prescription of bed rails for assistance in keeping a resident safely in her bed after she was found unresponsive with her head wedged between the mattress and bed rail during hourly rounds.[53] In *Schieber v. Mariner Post-Acute Network*, the plaintiff, on behalf of her mother's estate, alleged that the facility and staff caused the resident's death by failing to obtain permission to use a physical restraint and by failing to remove the restraint when the resident became combative and agitated.[54]

Counsel litigating these difficult restraint cases should ensure that experts are retained early to evaluate the presence of and appropriateness of any physical or chemical restraints in the long-term care setting.

Medication Errors and Drug Diversion

Many long-term care residents are prescribed one or more medications from the inception of their residencies.[55] These may include Coumadin for heart or circulatory conditions, psychotropics for Alzheimer's or dementia, antibiotics for infection, pain medication, and a variety of others. Medical administration cases usually take one of two forms: allegations that there was a failure to properly monitor or administer medication, or allegations that a caregiver diverted—or stole—a medication meant for a resident.

For example, in *Continued Care, Inc. v. Fournet*, the heirs of a nursing home resident filed suit alleging negligent supervision of the director of nursing, who allegedly stole or diverted the resident's pain medication, causing unnecessary or increased pain or suffering to the resident.[56] In *Williams v. Alvista Healthcare Center, Inc.*, the children of a nursing home resident brought a wrongful death action stemming from the nursing home staff's alleged failure to administer prescribed medication after the resident complained of chest pains and was diagnosed with coronary insufficiency.[57]

When evaluating issues of medication administration, counsel and their experts should pay particular attention to the resident's physician orders, the medication administration record (MAR), nurse's notes containing medication information, and controlled substance records.

---

53. Estate of Hendrickson *ex rel.* Hendrickson v. Genesis Health Venture, Inc., 565 S.E.2d 254 (N.C. Ct. App. 2002).

54. Schieber v. Mariner Post-Acute Network, No. 2003-18381, 2005 WL 3831929 (Tex. Dist. Oct. 14, 2005).

55. *See* Elaine Lau & Lisa R. Dolovich, *Drug-Related Problems in Elderly General Practice Patients Receiving Pharmaceutical Care*, 13 Int. J. Pharm. Pract. 165 (2005).

56. Continued Care, Inc. v. Fournet, 979 S.W.2d 419 (Tex. Ct. App. 1998).

57. Williams v. Alvista Healthcare Ctr., Inc., 283 Ga. App. 613 (Ct. App. 2007).

Conclusion

Litigating a medical malpractice case in the long-term care sphere requires a heightened level of attention to detail and an understanding of the comorbidities that give rise to the need for long-term care. Mastery of the applicable regulations, standards of care, and subject medical record will aid counsel's advocacy.

3

PHARMACEUTICAL PRODUCT LIABILITY LITIGATION

Tamar Kelber and Daniel Kennedy

The primary differences between pharmaceutical product liability litigation and traditional products litigation arise from the federal Food and Drug Administration (FDA) regulation of pharmaceuticals and the learned intermediary doctrine. Although there are important differences in applicable regulations, the FDA regulates both pharmaceuticals and medical devices, and the learned intermediary doctrine has a similar application in both contexts. As such, there are many similarities between pharmaceutical and medical device litigation.

This chapter provides an overview of FDA regulation of pharmaceuticals, discusses the claims most commonly asserted in pharmaceutical product liability litigation, and concludes with a discussion of other issues seen in the pharmaceutical context. The next chapter focuses on medical devices and the specific issues that arise in device cases.

Background: The FDA Approval Process

The FDA sits within the Department of Health and Human Services and regulates food, drugs, tobacco, medical devices, and biologics. The FDA's Center for Drug Evaluation and Research (CDER) regulates over-the-counter and prescription drugs. The FDA's Center for Devices and Radiologic Health (CDRH) regulates medical devices. Finally, the FDA's Center for Biologics Evaluation and Research regulates therapeutic substances derived from animal products or other biologic sources, such as vaccines, blood components, gene therapy, and recombinant products. Some therapeutics are "combination products," which fall under the purview of two review divisions; for those therapeutics, regulatory authority is shared by the two divisions. For example, a product that is a combination drug with delivery device would be regulated jointly by CDER and CDRH as a combination product.[1] The FDA's Office of Combination Products coordinates and oversees this regulation.

1. While it is beyond the purview of this chapter, litigation regarding biologics raises many similar issues to litigation regarding pharmaceuticals. The regulations governing biologics can be found at 21 C.F.R. § 600 *et seq.*

Regulations governing pharmaceuticals are found in subchapters C (Drugs: General) and D (Drugs for Human Use) of Title 21 of the Code of Federal Regulations. The FDA periodically issues "Guidance for Industry" documents that provide helpful information regarding its interpretation and application of the regulations. Guidance can be found on the FDA's website at http://www.fda.gov/Drugs/GuidanceComplianceRegulatoryInformation/Guidances/default.htm.[2]

Development and marketing of a pharmaceutical product is a long, multilayered process. It is important for a lawyer handling pharmaceutical product liability cases to have a working understanding of that process. Once a compound is developed, the "sponsor" tests the compound for toxicity on multiple species of animals and develops a plan for testing it on human subjects. The sponsor submits the results of the animal testing and plans for human testing to the FDA in an Investigational New Drug Application (IND). There are three phases of testing on human subjects. Phase 1 evaluates the drug's side effects and how the drug is metabolized. Phase 2 tests the drug's efficacy in patients with the condition or disease that the drug is intended to treat. Thereafter, the sponsor meets with the FDA and develops a plan for Phase 3. In Phase 3, the drug is tested in thousands of human subjects who receive the drug in different dosages.

Next, the sponsor submits a New Drug Application (NDA). The NDA includes summary information regarding the prior phase of testing, manufacturing information, and the company's proposed labeling. In the NDA, the sponsor must demonstrate that the drug is safe and effective, that the benefits outweigh the risks, and that there are adequate manufacturing methods and controls. If the FDA accepts the NDA for filing, it assigns a review team to evaluate the submission. The FDA also reviews the proposed labeling and inspects the sponsor's proposed manufacturing facility. Thereafter, the FDA issues either an approval letter or a response letter to the sponsor. The response letter may direct the sponsor to perform additional testing. After approval, the drug's sponsor must submit periodic safety updates to the FDA. The FDA also receives and reviews Adverse Event Reports (AERs) directly from physicians and consumers through its MedWatch system.

While the FDA does not regulate the practice of medicine, it does approve drugs for particular indications. The NDA must demonstrate the drug's safety and efficacy for the indications for which the sponsor seeks approval. Once approved, the sponsor may only promote the drug for the approved indication. Use for anything other than an approved indication is deemed "off-label." To obtain the FDA's approval for a new indication or dose, a sponsor submits a Supplemental New Drug Application (sNDA). A generic drug manufacturer submits an Abbreviated New Drug Application (ANDA) for a generic version of an approved drug.

---

2. The FDA website is an invaluable resource for pharmaceutical product liability litigation. For example, approval histories, labeling, and FDA correspondence are all available on the Drugs@FDA page of the website. *See* DRUGS@FDA, http://www.accessdata.fda.gov/scripts/cder/drugsatfda/index.cfm.

The sponsor must submit all promotional materials for a drug to the FDA's Office of Prescription Drug Promotion (OPDP).[3] OPDP reviews promotional material to ensure that it is truthful, is not misleading, includes all material information about a drug, and includes "fair balance," presenting a balanced picture of risk and benefit.[4] OPDP may send an "untitled letter" regarding promotional material that does not meet its criteria. OPDP will send a "warning letter" for regulatory violations, providing detail about the violation and OPDP's desired corrective action.[5] The FDA considers warning letters discretionary, and as such the FDA is not required to take regulatory action if a company does not comply with a warning letter to OPDP's satisfaction.

FDA-approved drugs must be accompanied by a package insert, which provides "a summary of the essential scientific information needed for the safe and effective use of the drug."[6] If the FDA determines that direct written instructions to the patient are necessary, the FDA may require the sponsor to provide patients with a medication guide (sometimes also referred to as a patient package insert).[7]

Claims

When an individual is harmed by ingestion of a pharmaceutical product, the traditional remedy is a claim against the product manufacturer for failure to warn, design defect, or defect under a state statutory scheme. Nonetheless, plaintiffs often also assert claims against suppliers, prescribers, and other intermediaries. Similarly, they often make claims under a variety of legal theories, including strict liability, negligence, and breach of warranty. The following sections discuss those claims most often asserted in pharmaceutical litigation.

Strict Liability

Strict liability refers to liability imposed without proof of a specific wrongful or negligent act or proof of wrongful intent. A drug manufacturer may be held strictly liable for injuries caused by a drug that is sold in a defective condition that renders it unreasonably dangerous to consumers. Strict liability may be imposed even if the manufacturer has "exercised all possible care in the preparation and sale"

3. OPDP was previously known as the Division of Drug Marketing, Advertising and Communications (DDMAC).

4. 21 C.F.R. § 202.1(e)(7).

5. Warning letters issued by year can be found at *Warning Letters and Notice of Violation Letters to Pharmaceutical Companies*, FDA, http://www.fda.gov/Drugs/GuidanceComplianceRegulatoryInformation/EnforcementActivitiesbyFDA/WarningLettersandNoticeofViolationLetterstoPharmaceuticalCompanies/ (last updated Apr. 2, 2020).

6. *See* 21 C.F.R. § 201.56(a)(1).

7. The criteria for requiring a medication guide are set forth in 21 C.F.R. § 208.1(c).

of the drug and even though the plaintiff has not purchased it directly from the manufacturer.[8]

While the specific elements and proof required for a strict liability claim may vary among jurisdictions, such claims are generally predicated upon *Restatement (Second) of Torts* § 402A, which provides:

> (1) One who sells any product in a defective condition unreasonably dangerous to the user or consumer or to his property is subject to liability for physical harm thereby caused to the ultimate user or consumer, or to his property, if:
> (a) The seller is engaged in the business of selling such a product;
> (b) It is expected to and does reach the user or consumer without substantial change in the condition in which it is sold.
> (2) The rule stated in subsection (1) applies although:
> (a) The seller has exercised all possible care in the preparation and sale of his product; and
> (b) The user or consumer has not bought the product from or entered into any contractual relation with the seller.

A drug may be found to be defective and unreasonably dangerous due to a defect in its design or manufacture or because it is not accompanied by adequate warnings.

Some products cannot be made completely safe for all consumers, even when used as intended. Recognizing this, courts and commentators acknowledged that strict liability may not attach to products determined to be "unavoidably unsafe."[9] In discussing this concept, the *Restatement (Second) of Torts* specifically identified drugs as a category of products to which this description may apply. As discussed below, although the majority of jurisdictions hold that comment k applies to prescription drugs, some courts have reached different conclusions.

Failure to Warn

The most common theory of strict liability asserted against drug manufacturers is based on the alleged failure to provide adequate warnings concerning the risks or side effects of a drug. Warnings, instructions, and other information about prescription and nonprescription drugs are contained in a "package insert" that accompanies a particular medication and may also be included in labels, advertisements, or other promotional materials. The FDA regulates the content of package inserts, which generally contain information about (1) how a drug works in the body; (2) "indications," or uses for which a drug has been approved by the FDA; (3) "contraindications," or situations in which a drug should not be used; (4) warnings about possible side effects; (5) proper dosage and administration of

8. *See* RESTATEMENT (SECOND) OF TORTS § 402A (1965).
9. *Id.* at cmt. k.

the drug; (6) precautions for safe use of the drug; (7) adverse reactions observed in studies of the drug; and (8) the potential for abuse and dependence (if applicable).[10] Failure to warn claims often focus on what is (or is not) included in labels, package inserts, or advertising or promotional materials.[11]

To prevail on a failure to warn claim, a plaintiff generally must show the existence of a duty to warn owed by the manufacturer to the plaintiff; a breach of the duty, as where a manufacturer knew or should have known that the warnings and other information it provided about the risks and side effects associated with a drug were inaccurate, unclear, or insufficient; and a causal connection between the breach and the plaintiff's injury. The following paragraphs discuss issues that may lurk in proving each of these elements.

The scope of a prescription drug manufacturer's duty to warn varies little across jurisdictions. In New York, for example, a manufacturer's duty is to warn of all potential dangers associated with its prescription drug that it knew or, in the exercise of reasonable care, should have known to exist.[12] Manufacturers must also conduct adequate research and testing before marketing their drugs.

In providing warnings, manufacturers are generally held to the standard of scientific knowledge prevailing at the time a drug is sold, rather than the standard prevailing at the time of trial. Thus, a manufacturer generally does not have a duty to warn of risks about which it did not know and could not reasonably have known at the time of sale. However, drug manufacturers are held to the standard of care of an expert in their respective fields and have a continuing duty to keep informed of emerging knowledge concerning their products and an obligation to update medical providers as to potential adverse effects.

In most jurisdictions, a manufacturer's duty to provide warnings and instructions about prescription drugs is satisfied by providing proper warnings to prescribing physicians, who act as "learned intermediaries" between the manufacturer and consumers. The manufacturer's duty to warn does not extend to the patient for whom the drug is prescribed because the patient is not presumed to have the expertise necessary to appreciate the significance of the risks involved and to weigh those risks against the potential benefits offered by a drug. Accordingly, a manufacturer can be shielded from liability by providing adequate warnings about risks and side effects to physicians, who in turn have an obligation to weigh the risks and benefits of the drug and provide sufficient information and warnings to

10. Labeling requirements for prescription drugs and biological products are listed in 21 C.F.R. § 201.57.

11. Failure to warn cases involving generic drugs present unique challenges because a generic drug's label is dictated by the label of the corresponding branded drug. *See* 21 U.S.C. § 355(j)(2)(A)(v). Consequently, failure to warn claims against generic drug manufacturers are preempted. Mut. Pharm. Co., Inc. v. Bartlett, 570 U.S. 472 (2013).

12. *See* Martin v. Hacker, 628 N.E.2d 1308 (N.Y. 1993).

patients to enable them to make an informed choice about whether to use it. This principle is referred to as the learned intermediary doctrine.[13]

Plaintiffs have attempted—with limited success to date—to circumvent the learned intermediary doctrine and extend the manufacturer's duty directly to consumers. Several decisions in the 1980s recognized a limited exception to the doctrine for manufacturers of oral contraceptives.[14] More recently, as prescription drug manufacturers have increased the amount of advertising directed at consumers, some courts have questioned whether the doctrine should continue to preclude the extension of a manufacturer's duty to consumers.[15] Some have carved out exceptions to the doctrine where direct-to-consumer advertising is at issue.[16] The *Restatement (Third) of Torts* has also recognized that "direct warnings and instructions to patients are warranted for drugs that are dispensed or administered to patients without the personal intervention or evaluation of a health-care provider."[17] This issue requires jurisdiction-specific research regarding the application of the doctrine early in the case.

The second element of a failure to warn claim requires a plaintiff to prove a breach of the manufacturer's duty. The breach analysis can involve examination of the manufacturer's testing and other efforts to uncover risks and side effects associated with a prescription drug. It can also require examination of a drug's label, package insert, or other advertising or promotional materials. In determining whether a warning is adequate, courts must analyze not only the meaning and content of the warning's language but also its form and manner of expression.

13. The doctrine does not apply to medications that are available to consumers without a prescription, such as over-the-counter pain relievers.

14. *See* McDonald v. Ortho Pharm. Corp., 475 N.E.2d 65 (Mass. 1985); Stephens v. G.D. Searle & Co., 602 F. Supp. 379 (E.D. Mich. 1979); Odgers v. Ortho Pharm. Corp., 609 F. Supp. 867 (E.D. Mich. 1985).

15. *See, e.g.*, State *ex rel.* Johnson & Johnson Corp. v. Karl, 647 S.E.2d 899 (W. Va. 2007), *superseded by statute as stated in* J.C. by and through Michelle C. v. Pfizer, Inc., 814 S.E.2d 234 (W. Va. 2018) (acknowledging West Virginia legislature's enactment of statute codifying learned intermediary doctrine in 2016); Rimbert v. Eli Lilly & Co., 577 F. Supp. 2d 1174, 1218 (D.N.M. 2008), *aff'd in part, rev'd in part*, 647 F.3d 1247 (10th Cir. 2011) (denying summary judgment, reasoning that "a dramatically increased marketing directed to consumers and the use of the interest [sic] by consumers to conduct their own medical research—would persuade the Supreme Court of New Mexico that the justification for the learned-intermediary doctrine is quickly becoming, if not already the case, outdated").

16. Perez v. Wyeth Labs. Inc., 734 A.2d 1245 (N.J. 1999) ("We believe that when mass marketing of prescription drugs seeks to influence a patient's choice of a drug, a pharmaceutical manufacturer that makes direct claims to consumers for the efficacy of its product should not be unqualifiedly relieved of a duty to provide proper warnings of the dangers or side effects of the product."); *but see* DiBartolo v. Abbott Labs., 914 F. Supp. 2d 601 (S.D.N.Y. 2012) ("Even in a world with widespread [direct-to-consumer] advertising, however, physicians continue to fulfill the core functions that underlie [the learned intermediary doctrine]: they evaluate a patient's needs, assess the risks and benefits of available drugs and then prescribe a drug, advising the patient of its risks and possible side effects. The physician therefore remains an 'informed intermediary' to whom manufacturers should direct prescription drug warnings.").

17. Restatement (Third) of Torts: Prods. Liab. § 6 cmt. e (1998).

Whether a warning is adequate is generally considered an issue of fact, but warnings can be found adequate as a matter of law if they provide specific detailed information on the risks associated with a particular drug.

Courts have considered several factors when analyzing the adequacy of a warning, including whether it is accurate, clear, and consistent on its face and whether it portrays with sufficient intensity the risk involved in taking the drug.[18] In general, a warning will be found accurate where it correctly and completely conveys up-to-date information as to the drug's known risks and side effects. A warning will be found sufficiently clear if it communicates those risks and side effects in direct and unequivocal language that adequately conveys the risk. However, an otherwise clear warning can be obscured by inconsistencies or contradictory statements in other portions of the package insert that address the same side effect or by language that lessens the intensity of a warning contained in an earlier section. Such inconsistencies may be sufficient to create a question of fact as to the warning's adequacy, although if the language of a particular warning is precise, direct, unequivocal, and sufficiently forceful, it may offset inconsistencies elsewhere in the insert.[19]

Finally, to establish proximate cause, a plaintiff must prove that had appropriate warnings been given, the treating physician would not have prescribed the drug or would have discontinued its use.[20] Even if a warning is inadequate or misrepresents a particular risk, a plaintiff must still connect the inadequacy of the warning to his injury. Some jurisdictions recognize a rebuttable presumption that a treating physician would have factored an adequate warning into the risk-benefit analysis in deciding whether to prescribe a drug. This "heeding presumption" does not, however, extend so far as to presume that the drug would not have been prescribed.[21] Thus, if the patient's physician is independently aware of a potential risk or side effect associated with a particular drug, the failure of a warning to address that risk adequately will not be a proximate cause of the patient's injury.[22] Likewise, if the patient's physician testifies that the absence or inadequacy of a warning did not affect the prescribing decision, the required causal nexus between the warning and the patient's injuries will likely be found absent. Proof of causation will also require testimony from a medical expert that the plaintiff's adverse medical effects were proximately caused by the drug.

Design Defect

Another theory of strict liability asserted against pharmaceutical manufacturers is defective design. The design of a drug refers to its formulation and chemical

18. Golod v. Hoffman La Roche, 964 F. Supp. 841, 853 (S.D.N.Y. 1997).
19. *See* Martin v. Hacker, 628 N.E.2d 1308, 1313 (N.Y. 1993).
20. *Golod*, 964 F. Supp. at 857.
21. Ingram v. Novartis Pharm. Corp., 888 F. Supp. 2d 1241 (W.D. Okla. 2012).
22. *See, e.g.*, Krasnopolsky v. Warner-Lambert Co., 799 F. Supp. 1342 (E.D.N.Y. 1992).

composition. Under the framework for strict liability set forth under *Restatement (Second) of Torts* § 402A, a product's design may be defective if a feature or characteristic of the design renders the product unreasonably dangerous to consumers. In considering the possibility of asserting a defective design claim against a drug manufacturer, practitioners should be aware of two issues that have been the subject of considerable discussion by courts and commentators.

The first issue concerns the impact of the unavoidably unsafe doctrine set forth in comment k to section 402A. The doctrine provides that products that are "incapable of being made safe for their intended and ordinary use" are nonetheless considered not to be defective or unreasonably dangerous so long as they are "properly prepared and accompanied by proper directions and warning."[23] All prescription drugs possess substantial treatment benefits as well as potential risks that are inherent and unavoidable. Jurisdictions that apply section 402A have come to different conclusions concerning the effect of the doctrine on design defect claims involving drugs.[24]

Some jurisdictions have applied the doctrine generally to prescription drugs so as to confer immunity from liability for design defects so long as the drug is properly prepared and accompanied by adequate directions and warnings. These courts have emphasized that prescription drugs are approved for distribution by the FDA and serve an important public interest in alleviating pain and prolonging life. As stated in comment k, a manufacturer or seller of a properly manufactured and marketed drug should not be held strictly liable "merely because he has undertaken to supply the public with an apparently useful and desirable product, attended with a known but apparently reasonable risk."[25] (Note, however, that jurisdictions that accord unavoidably unsafe immunity to manufacturers of prescription drugs may not accord the same treatment to manufacturers of over-the-counter medications.)

Other jurisdictions have rejected the notion that prescription drugs should be deemed unavoidably unsafe as a matter of law. Many of these jurisdictions treat comment k as an affirmative defense and subject prescription drugs to a case-by-case risk-benefit analysis used to evaluate design defect claims for other products. Under this analysis, the risks inherent in the use of the drug are weighed against the drug's efficacy. Courts in these jurisdictions analyze a variety of factors in balancing risks versus benefit. Whether a reasonable or safer alternative design is available is often an important factor in this analysis.[26] A few jurisdictions have not adopted comment k and simply treat prescription drugs like other products.

---

23. Restatement (Second) of Torts § 402A cmt. k (1965).

24. *See generally* Joanne Rhoton Galbreath, *Products Liability: What Is an "Unavoidably Unsafe" Product*, 70 A.L.R. 4th 16 (1989).

25. Restatement (Second) of Torts § 402A cmt. k.

26. *See, e.g.*, Booker v. Johnson & Johnson, 54 F. Supp. 3d 868, 873 (N.D. Ohio 2014) (applying Georgia law).

The second issue arises in jurisdictions where a plaintiff must establish the existence of a suitable alternative design to prevail on a design defect claim. In these jurisdictions, strict liability claims premised on a theory of design defect may be preempted to the extent that they would require a manufacturer to change the composition or formulation of a drug that is not permitted under federal law.[27]

The *Restatement (Third) of Torts* introduced significant changes to the law governing design defect claims against makers of prescription drugs. Under section 6(c) of the *Restatement (Third)*, liability for a defective design may arise if the foreseeable risks of harm posed by a drug are "sufficiently great in relation to its foreseeable therapeutic benefits that reasonable health care providers, knowing of such foreseeable risks and therapeutic benefits, would not prescribe the drug . . . for any class of patients."[28] This formulation for design defect liability has been criticized for narrowing the scope of design defect theory and has not gained much traction in the courts as of this writing.[29]

At the end of the day, design defect claims are rarely viable against drug manufacturers because of the inherent risks associated with any prescription drug.

Manufacturing Defect

The third theory of strict liability asserted against drug manufacturers is manufacturing defect. Manufacturing defect claims generally require proof that the defendant manufactured a product that departs from its intended design in a manner that renders it unreasonably dangerous to consumers, the product left the manufacturer's control in a defective and unreasonably dangerous condition, and the product caused the plaintiff's injuries.

For pharmaceuticals, manufacturing defect claims often require proof that a particular dose or batch of a drug deviated materially in formulation or chemical composition from the manufacturing specifications or from otherwise identical batches of the drug in a manner that rendered the drug unreasonably dangerous.[30]

Manufacturing defects are usually attributable to failures in a manufacturer's quality control systems or processes. As with failure to warn and design defect claims, expert analysis and testimony are usually required to identify a deviation from the intended formulation or composition, and it can be difficult to connect that deviation to a flaw in the manufacturer's quality control system. These evidentiary hurdles and the litigation costs to overcome them result in manufacturing defect claims rarely being pursued. In addition, manufacturing defect claims are rarely successful, in part because quality control systems are closely regulated,

27. Chapter 4 discusses the defense of preemption in claims regarding medical devices in greater detail.

28. Restatement (Third) of Torts § 6(c) (1998).

29. *See* Freeman v. Hoffman-La Roche, Inc., 618 N.W.2d 827 (Neb. 2000).

30. Solomon v. Bristol-Myers Squibb Co., 916 F. Supp. 2d 556 (D.N.J. 2013).

production is largely automated, and manufacturer compliance with specifications has traditionally been high.

Negligence

Negligence is the most common theory of product liability alleged against manufacturers, distributors, and sellers of pharmaceutical products. To prevail under traditional principles of negligence, the plaintiff must prove that (1) the defendant owed a particular duty to the plaintiff related to the drug; (2) the defendant breached that duty; (3) the plaintiff took the drug; (4) the plaintiff suffered adverse medical effects; and (5) the adverse effects were proximately caused by the breach of duty.

Negligence claims may target a wide range of manufacturer action (or inaction) in the development, study, testing, manufacture, distribution, marketing, or sale of a particular drug. For example, a plaintiff may allege that a manufacturer failed to use ordinary care in testing a drug so as to detect a risk of unreasonable and dangerous side effects. A plaintiff may also allege that the manufacturer breached its duty to warn physicians, patients, or others about the risk of adverse effects associated with the use of a drug or the nature, duration, or severity of those adverse effects. Negligence claims may also target a manufacturer's testing, analysis, and promotion of a drug after it is introduced to the market. Many of the proof considerations discussed above with regard to strict liability failure to warn claims are also pertinent to establishing liability under negligence.

Breach of Warranty

Claims for breach of express or implied warranty have also been asserted against drug manufacturers and sellers. Liability under warranty principles may exist if a plaintiff can show that a manufacturer or seller implicitly or expressly made a representation about a drug that was false or misleading. Like strict liability, liability under warranty does not require a plaintiff to demonstrate negligence on the part of a manufacturer. However, because of the learned intermediary doctrine, the lack of privity between patient and manufacturer, and the fact that most patients do not read and rely on prescription drug labels, warranty claims typically do not withstand motions for summary judgment.

Implied Warranties

Most jurisdictions recognize two implied warranties in the sale of goods set forth in the Uniform Commercial Code—the implied warranties of merchantability and fitness for a particular purpose.

As applied to pharmaceutical products, the implied warranty of merchantability assures consumers that the drug product is reasonably suitable for the ordinary use for which it is purchased and sold.[31] A manufacturer breaches this warranty when a defect in its drug makes it unfit or unsuitable for the ordinary treatment purposes for which the drug was intended. The defect that renders the drug unsuitable for its intended purpose may be in its design, in its manufacture, or by virtue of the manufacturer's failure to warn of known potential adverse effects in the taking of the drug. As this formulation suggests, many of the same proof considerations applicable to strict liability failure to warn claims apply to claims alleging breach of the implied warranty of merchantability.

The second widely recognized implied warranty is the warranty of fitness for a particular purpose. In the context of a pharmaceutical product, this warranty can arise as a matter of law where a manufacturer or seller of a drug has reason to know of a particular treatment purpose for which the drug is required and that the plaintiff is relying on the skill or judgment of the manufacturer or seller to provide a drug suitable for that purpose.[32] A claim for breach of this warranty is based on statements or representations made by a defendant (in a label or package insert) that impliedly warrant that a drug is fit for the particular purpose for which the drug was prescribed. Such statements or representations need not constitute an express warranty but may contain language that a physician relies upon in prescribing the drug, thus impliedly warranting that the drug is fit to treat the plaintiff's malady. A manufacturer or other seller breaches this warranty where the drug fails to function properly in treating the plaintiff's illness or is not fit for that treatment purpose for which it was prescribed. Such lack of fitness can arise, for example, where the manufacturer fails to warn of the adverse effects a plaintiff experiences after taking the drug.

Express Warranty

In addition to the implied warranties discussed above, practitioners should also consider whether statements in a drug's label, package insert, or other advertising or promotional materials could support a claim for breach of an express warranty. Under section 2-313 of the UCC, an express warranty may be created by an "affirmation of fact or promise" about a product, by a description of the product, or by a sample of the product.

Pharmaceutical manufacturers rarely make representations in a drug's label, package insert, or other advertising or promotional materials that could be construed as express warranties about a drug's efficacy, safety, or lack of side effects. For this reason, careful consideration should be given to determining whether any statements attributable to a manufacturer meet the applicable legal standard for an express warranty. Absent the required level of specificity and clarity, a breach of express warranty claim will almost certainly be dismissed before trial.

---

31. *See* U.C.C. § 2-314.
32. *See id.* § 2-315.

Fraud/Misrepresentation

In addition to the theories of product liability discussed above, plaintiffs often assert common-law claims for fraud and misrepresentation against pharmaceutical manufacturers. Such claims typically focus on negligent or intentional misrepresentations—affirmative false or misleading statements—or a failure to disclose material information attributable to a manufacturer concerning the safety, efficacy, risks, or benefits of a drug.

A plaintiff pursuing a fraud or misrepresentation claim must generally establish that (1) the defendant made a representation of fact or failed to disclose information where it had a duty to do so; (2) the information at issue was material to the prescribing decision; (3) the representation or omission was made falsely, with knowledge of its falsity, or with reckless disregard for its truth; (4) the representation or omission was made with intent to mislead another into relying upon it; (5) the plaintiff (or her physician) justifiably relied on the representation or concealment; and (6) the plaintiff's injury was proximately caused by the reliance.[33] A manufacturer may have a duty to disclose only if it has a fiduciary or other particular relationship with a consumer.[34]

As with strict liability and warranty claims, fraud and misrepresentation claims typically focus on the contents of a drug's package insert, label, or other advertisement and promotional materials. However, the facts underlying a particular case may give rise to claims for other fraudulent conduct, such as

- submitting false or "doctored" documents concerning clinical trials of a drug to the FDA;
- failing to disclose or concealing from the FDA negative results of clinical trial studies;
- failing to disclose material limitations in premarket testing or postmarket monitoring that prevent the manufacturer from adequately determining the safety and efficacy of a drug;
- promoting the sale and use of a drug for purposes not specifically approved by the FDA; or
- improperly encouraging off-label uses of a prescription drug by providing financial or other inducements to physicians to prescribe the drug for those uses.

This necessary focus on the content of the FDA-approved labeling creates a generally insurmountable obstacle to asserting fraud claims. Because the FDA is the arbiter of the label, a claim that the label was misleading amounts to either an attack on the FDA or an argument that the manufacturer committed fraud on

33. *See* Rheinfrank v. Abbott Labs., Inc., 119 F. Supp. 3d 749, 787 (S.D. Ohio 2015).

34. Riggins v. Ortho McNeil Pharm., Inc., 51 F. Supp. 3d 708 (N.D. Ohio 2014) (applying California law) (plaintiff could not establish fiduciary relationship where she had no contact with manufacturer before being prescribed birth control patch); Moretti v. Wyeth, Inc., 579 Fed. Appx. 563 (9th Cir. 2014) (applying Nevada law).

the FDA. As discussed more fully in Chapter 4, claims for fraud on the FDA are preempted.[35] And the Food, Drug, and Cosmetics Act (FDCA) expressly prohibits private causes of action for violation of the FDCA or FDA implementing regulations.

Statutory Causes of Action

Many states have consumer protection statutes that have received increasing attention in recent years. Violations of those statutes are often included in pharmaceutical product liability actions.[36] Like warranty claims, they are often vulnerable to early dismissal.

Plaintiffs sometimes try to circumvent the FDCA's prohibition on private rights of action by asserting claims for negligence per se. In other words, they argue that the defendant violated the FDCA or implementing regulations and that the violation constitutes negligence per se. Courts, however, have generally held that a negligence per se claim violates the prohibition on private rights of action.[37]

In addition, many states have product liability statutes that subsume common-law claims.[38] While the details of such statutes are beyond the purview of this chapter, many statutes track common-law failure to warn claims. Product liability statutes often expressly preclude other claims arising out of the same alleged injuries, which can be used in dispositive motions on other counts.[39]

Recoverable Damages

A wide variety of compensatory damages may be recovered in pharmaceutical product liability actions, including (1) the costs of past and anticipated future medical care and treatment required to treat the adverse effects suffered by the plaintiff; (2) past and anticipated lost wages, income, or earning capacity; (3) damages for past pain and suffering and for pain and suffering reasonably likely to occur in the future; (4) damages for permanent disfigurement, physical injury, or disability; (5) compensation for past and reasonably anticipated future mental, psychological, and emotional distress; and (6) damages for the plaintiff's loss of society, companionship, and consortium.[40] Where the patient dies as the result

35. *See* Buckman Co. v. Plaintiffs' Legal Comm., 531 U.S. 341, 350 (2001) ("State-law fraud-on-the-FDA claims inevitably conflict with the FDA's responsibility to police fraud consistently with the Agency's judgment and objectives.").

36. *See, e.g.*, Daniel J. Penofsky, *Products Liability of Pharmaceutical Manufacturers for Antipsychotic Drugs*, 126 Am. Jur. Trials 1 § 28 (2012).

37. *See, e.g.*, Rounds v. Genzyme Corp., No. 8:10–cv–2479–T–23TBM, 2010 WL 5297180 (M.D. Fla. Dec. 20, 2010), *aff'd*, 2011 WL 3925353 (11th Cir. 2011).

38. *See, e.g.*, Louisiana Products Liability Act, La. Rev. Stat. § 9:2800.51 *et seq.*

39. *See, e.g.*, *id.* § 2800.52 ("This Chapter establishes the exclusive theories of liability for manufacturers for damage caused by their products.").

40. For a comprehensive discussion of potentially recoverable damages in an action against a pharmaceutical manufacturer, see 126 Am. Jur. Trials §§ 40–43 (2012).

of taking a drug, additional damages that may be recovered include damages for wrongful death, funeral expenses, and loss of past and future financial support. Because pharmaceutical product liability cases almost always involve conditions for which the plaintiff or plaintiff's decedent received medical treatment, liens are often asserted by third-party healthcare providers and private and governmental payors for healthcare services.[41]

In addition to compensatory damages, punitive or exemplary damages may be recoverable in an action against a drug manufacturer. Such damages are not intended to compensate an injured plaintiff but rather are meant to punish a defendant for unlawful or outrageous conduct and to deter the defendant and others from engaging in similar conduct. State statutes and common law will usually govern the availability of punitive damages in actions against pharmaceutical manufacturers, the nature of the conduct required to support an award of punitive damages, and the procedures by which a claim for punitive damages is adjudicated. In addition to state law requirements, before imposing punitive damages awards, courts must consider "(1) the degree of reprehensibility of the defendant's misconduct; (2) the disparity between the actual or potential harm suffered by the plaintiff and the punitive damages award; and (3) the difference between the punitive damages awarded by the jury and the civil penalties authorized or imposed in comparable cases."[42] While the United States Supreme Court has not imposed a specific limit on the multiplier between compensatory and punitive damages, it has instructed that "[o]ur jurisprudence and the principles it has now established demonstrate, however, that, in practice, few awards exceeding a single-digit ratio between punitive and compensatory damages, to a significant degree, will satisfy due process."[43]

Notwithstanding the Supreme Court's direction in *State Farm*, recent pharmaceutical product liability litigation has resulted in punitive damages awards of staggering proportions. In *Allen et al. v. Takeda Pharmaceuticals North America, Inc. et al.*, for example, a jury issued a compensatory damages verdict of $1,475,000 and a punitive damages verdict of $9,000,000,000.[44] This verdict reflected a ratio of compensatory to punitive damages of 1:5,424 for one defendant and 1:8,136 for the other. On defendants' motion for a new trial, the court reduced the punitive damages to a ratio of 1:25, $36,875,000. It remains to be seen whether this case is an anomaly or suggests an expanding role for the scope of recoverable punitive damages. More recently, in *Murray v. Janssen Pharmaceuticals*, a jury awarded $8,000,000,000 in punitive damages to a plaintiff who developed gynecomastia

41. When settling pharmaceutical product liability claims, both plaintiff and defense must make sure that reporting obligations to potential lienholders are satisfied. The Medicare, Medicaid, and SCHIP Extension Act (MMSEA) requires defendants to report settlements to the Centers for Medicare & Medicaid Services (CMS). Penalties for noncompliance are large—$1,000 per claim per day.

42. State Farm Mut. Auto. Ins. Co. v. Campbell, 538 U.S. 408, 418 (2003) (citing BMW of N. Am., Inc. v. Gore, 517 U.S. 559, 575 (1996)).

43. *Id.* at 425.

44. Allen et al. v. Takeda Pharm. N. Am., Inc. et al., No. 6:11–md–2299, 2014 WL 5461859 (W.D. La. 2014).

after taking the antipsychotic drug Risperdal.[45] In that case, the court reduced the punitive damages award to $6,800,000, an amount equal to ten times the compensatory damages award.[46]

Procedural and Jurisdictional Issues

Removal

As with most product liability litigation, pharmaceutical product liability defendants typically prefer to litigate in federal court and plaintiffs in state court. Federal court jurisdiction is typically based on diversity of citizenship; thus plaintiffs seeking to stay in state court will often look for local defendants to include in the case. It is not unusual for a plaintiff to include a treating physician or pharmacy as a defendant in an effort to destroy diversity. If sufficient claims are not pled against the local defendant, the nonresident defendant may remove the case to federal court on a theory of "fraudulent joinder."[47] If the plaintiff does plead actionable claims against the local defendant, the nonresident defendant may still remove the action on the theory of "fraudulent misjoinder." Fraudulent misjoinder applies if the claims against the defendants are so different that there is no reasonable procedural basis to join the resident and nonresident defendant in the same action.[48]

Personal Jurisdiction in State Court Litigation

Historically, it was not uncommon for plaintiffs to combine the claims of a large number of pharmaceutical product liability plaintiffs from multiple states in state court before a single judge in a consolidated state court proceeding. While some of the plaintiffs resided in the forum state, courts would also exercise jurisdiction over claims brought by out-of-state plaintiffs against out-of-state manufacturers on the basis of the manufacturers' general operations within the state. In 2013, the Supreme Court's decision in *Daimler AG v. Bauman* sparked a shift in this jurisprudence.[49] In *Daimler*, the Supreme Court held that the trial court in California did not have jurisdiction over a suit between foreign parties. The Court reasoned that

45. Murray v. Janssen Pharm., 2019 WL 5295341 (Pa. Com. Pl.); Mihir Zaveri & Katie Thomas, *Johnson & Johnson Hit with $8 Billion Jury Verdict in Risperdal Suit*, N.Y. Times (Oct. 8, 2019), https://www.nytimes.com/2019/10/08/health/johnson-and-johnson-risperdal-verdict.html.

46. Max Mitchell, *Phila. Judge Knocks $8 Billion Risperdal Verdict Down to $6.8 Million*, The Legal Intelligencer (Jan. 17, 2020), https://www.law.com/thelegalintelligencer/2020/01/17/phila-judge-knocks-8-billion-risperdal-verdict-down-to-6-8-million/.

47. *In re* Zoloft (Sertraline Hydrochloride) Prods. Liab. Litig., 257 F. Supp. 3d 717 (E.D. Pa. 2017); Slater v. Hoffman–LaRoche, 771 F. Supp. 2d 524, 529 (E.D. Pa. 2011).

48. Tapscott v. MS Dealer Serv. Corp., 77 F.3d 1353 (11th Cir. 1996), *abrogated on other grounds by* Cohen v. Office Depot, Inc., 204 F.3d 1069 (11th Cir. 2000); *see also* Sullivan v. Calvert Mem. Hosp., 117 F. Supp. 3d 702 (D. Md. 2015) (severing and remanding claims against nondiverse healthcare provider).

49. 571 U.S. 117 (2014).

a court could exercise general jurisdiction only over a defendant with sufficient contacts to "render it at home there."[50]

In the pharmaceutical product liability context, the *Daimler* decision has been applied to pharmaceutical companies sued by nonresident plaintiffs in states where the company's activities are limited.[51] In the *Plavix* litigation, for example, 506 plaintiffs from various states sued Bristol-Myers Squibb and Sanofi-Aventis in Illinois state court. The court held that while it had specific jurisdiction over the defendants for the claims of the Illinois residents, it could not exercise general jurisdiction over the defendants for the claims of the 486 plaintiffs who did not reside in Illinois.[52] Importantly, the defendants' sales and distribution networks within the state did not create a sufficient basis for general jurisdiction. Thereafter, in *Bristol-Myers Squibb Co. v. Superior Court*, the Supreme Court examined specific jurisdiction in the coordinated California Plavix cases and held that state courts could not exercise jurisdiction over nonresident plaintiffs' claims against a pharmaceutical manufacturer because their claims lacked a sufficient link to the state.[53] Application of *Daimler* and *Bristol-Myers Squibb* may drastically reduce the size, and potentially the number, of coordinated state court proceedings in pharmaceutical product liability litigation.

Federal Multidistrict Litigation

While not unique to pharmaceutical product liability litigation, federal multidistrict litigation is often the epicenter of such litigation. The Judicial Panel on Multidistrict Litigation (JPML), which is comprised of seven sitting federal judges, convenes periodically to determine whether to assign multiple actions to the same federal judge for coordinated or consolidated pretrial proceedings.[54] The coordinated proceedings are called MDLs. The JPML will create an MDL for coordinated pretrial proceedings in federal court actions "involving one or more common questions of fact," if it determines that "transfers for such proceedings will be for the convenience of parties and witnesses and will promote the just and efficient conduct of such actions."[55] With input from the parties, the JPML selects the judge to preside over the MDL (the "transferee" judge).

50. *Id.* at 136.

51. *See In re* Plavix Related Cases, No. 2012 L 5688 (Cook Cnty. Cir. Ct. Aug. 11, 2014), *available at* http://www.cookcountycourt.org/Portals/0/Law%20Divison/Plavix/Plavix.5.28.15.PDF.

52. *Id.* at 9–11. A court may exercise "specific" personal jurisdiction over a defendant for claims arising out of the defendant's contacts with the forum. If there is no specific jurisdiction, a court may exercise "general" personal jurisdiction over any claims against a defendant who is at home in that forum.

53. Bristol-Myers Squibb Co. v. Super. Ct., 137 S. Ct. 1773 (2017).

54. 28 U.S.C. § 1407; *see Overview of Panel*, JUDICIAL PANEL ON MULTIDIST. LITIG., https://www.jpml.uscourts.gov/overview-panel-0 (last visited Oct. 1, 2020).

55. 28 U.S.C. § 1407(a).

MDL consolidation has become routine for pharmaceutical product liability litigation.[56] If a case is filed in or removed to federal court and it involves common questions of fact, i.e., alleges injury from the same pharmaceutical product, with a pending MDL, any party may file a "tag-along notice" with the JPML.[57] The JPML then issues a Conditional Transfer Order (CTO).[58] Thereafter, any other parties have seven days to file a notice of opposition.[59] The opposing party then files a motion to vacate the CTO, which is briefed and heard by the full JPML at its next hearing session.[60]

At the beginning of an MDL, the court appoints liaison and lead counsel on both sides of the bar. The plaintiffs' leadership is known as the Plaintiff Steering Committee (PSC). Once a case is transferred to an MDL, plaintiffs are typically required to complete standard discovery documents known as Plaintiff Fact Sheets (PFS) and execute authorizations for the defendants to collect relevant medical records.[61] Defendants are often required to submit corresponding Defendant Fact Sheets (DFS) that address the defendants' contacts, if any, with the plaintiff's healthcare providers. MDLs sometimes include master pleadings and a prescribed format for individual "short-form" complaints.

Common experts are often disclosed and *Daubert* motions briefed and argued before the MDL judge. It is also not unusual for an MDL judge to coordinate with judges overseeing consolidated state court proceedings. The MDL judge may also hold a bellwether trial before terminating the MDL. While the MDL judge has jurisdiction over all transferred actions for pretrial proceedings, the judge has jurisdiction for trials only over cases filed in the district in which the judge sits.[62] Upon completion of the MDL, the MDL judge remands individual cases to the district where they were filed (the "transferor" jurisdictions).[63] Often the MDL terminates with a global settlement of the plaintiffs' claims.

Pharmaceutical product liability litigation is characterized by lengthy and voluminous discovery and complex medical and scientific issues. While this sometimes makes a pharmaceutical case daunting, the coordination available through multidistrict litigation simplifies the case for the individual litigant.

---

56. In contrast, there is virtually no class action litigation of pharmaceutical product liability claims. There are too many individual issues and variations in state law to make class action litigation feasible. *See In re* Rhone-Poulenc Rorer, 51 F.3d 1293 (7th Cir. 1995) (granting mandamus petition and ordering district court to decertify nationwide product liability class). Class action litigation is discussed in detail in Chapter 4.

57. JPML R. 7.1(a).

58. *Id.* R. 7.1(b).

59. *Id.* R. 7.1(c).

60. *Id.* R. 7.1(f).

61. The Health Insurance Portability and Accountability Act of 1996 imposes limitations on the parties' collection of medical records.

62. Lexecon, Inc. v. Milberg Weiss Bershad Hynes & Lerach, 523 U.S. 26 (1998).

63. Litigants may also file a motion to remand an individual case to the transferor court before the MDL concludes.

Conclusion

Pharmaceutical cases present many of the same legal issues as other product liability litigation. The majority of the unique issues stem from the FDA's oversight of pharmaceutical drug development and promotion and the role of the learned intermediary. As such, understanding the regulatory framework and regulatory history of the pharmaceutical drug at issue and developing the factual record of the prescriber's knowledge are essential for the successful handling of a pharmaceutical product liability case.

4

MEDICAL DEVICE LITIGATION: THEORIES OF LIABILITY AND COMMON DEFENSES

Samuel L. Felker and Sarah Murray

Medical device litigation is a specialized area of products liability law. While many of the guiding principles are common to both medical device litigation and more generalized products liability litigation, the heavy overlay of federal regulation creates liability theories and defenses that are unique to medical device litigation. To be effective, the medical device litigator must understand the basic federal framework for approval, labeling, and monitoring of medical devices. Although a detailed discussion of the federal regulations governing medical devices is outside the scope of this chapter, a brief overview of the regulatory system will provide context for the exploration of issues related to medical device litigation. Following this overview, this chapter will address liability theories, defenses, and damages common to medical device cases.

Overview of Federal Regulation of Medical Devices

The U.S. Food and Drug Administration (FDA) regulates companies that manufacture medical devices sold in the United States. A medical device is "any instrument, apparatus, implement, machine, contrivance, implant, in vitro reagent or similar article . . . intended for use in the diagnosis, cure, mitigation, treatment or prevention of disease . . . which does not achieve its intended purpose by chemical action and need not be metabolized for achieving its purpose."[1] Medical devices are regulated by the Food, Drug, and Cosmetic Act (FDCA).[2] When the Medical Device Amendments (MDA) were enacted in 1976, the FDCA was amended and "swept back some state obligations and imposed a regime of detailed federal oversight" for medical devices.[3]

The FDCA established three classes of medical devices, with regulatory control increasing with each classification. Devices labeled Class I are devices that are

1. 21 C.F.R. § 312.1(a).
2. 21 U.S.C. §§ 301–399.
3. Riegel v. Medtronic, Inc., 552 U.S. 312, 316 (2008).

not of substantial importance to health and that do not present an unreasonable risk of injury or illness. Examples of Class I devices include enema kits and elastic bandages. Class II devices are devices that necessitate performance standards to ensure they are safely and effectively used. Examples of Class II devices are powered wheelchairs and some pregnancy kits. Class III devices are devices to be used in supporting or sustaining human life, devices that are of substantial importance in preventing impairment of human health, or devices that present a potential risk of illness or injury. Examples of Class III devices are implantable pacemakers and breast implants. Most Class II and all Class III devices must receive regulatory clearance by the FDA before they can be marketed in the United States.

There are two types of FDA regulatory clearance: the 510(k) process for clearance of devices that were on the market when the MDA passed or that are substantially equivalent to approved devices on the market; and the more extensive Premarket Approval process, which involves scientific and regulatory review to evaluate the safety and effectiveness of Class III medical devices. The vast majority of devices are cleared by the FDA under the streamlined 510(k) process whereby the manufacturer submits to the FDA a Premarket Notification containing detailed information about the device. The 510(k) filing must demonstrate that the device is substantially equivalent to one legally sold in the United States before May 28, 1976, or to a device that the FDA has authorized to be on the market. A product is substantially equivalent to another device when it has the same intended use and the same technological characteristics, or when it has the same intended use and different technological characteristics but does not raise new questions of safety and effectiveness and is at least as safe as the products already on the market. A manufacturer cannot commercially distribute a device until the FDA provides a letter of substantial equivalence.

Unlike the 510(k) process, the Premarket Approval process requires the manufacturer to submit scientific evidence demonstrating reasonable assurance of safety and effectiveness for the device's intended use. Approval for a Premarket Approval application (PMA) requires a determination by the FDA that the application contains enough scientific evidence to assure that the device is safe and effective for its intended use. While the FDA regulations provide a 180-day period for review, the review period is normally longer. Before approving or denying a PMA, the appropriate FDA advisory committee may review the PMA at a public meeting and provide the FDA with the committee's recommendation on whether the FDA should approve the submission. After the FDA notifies the applicant that the PMA has been approved or denied, a notice is published on the Internet (1) announcing the data on which the decision is based and (2) providing interested persons an opportunity to petition FDA within 30 days for reconsideration of the decision. A Class III device that fails to meet PMA requirements is considered to be adulterated under section 501(f) of the FDCA and cannot be marketed.

The FDA allows investigational device exemptions under which a device can be used in a clinical study so that the manufacturer can collect the data on the safety and effectiveness of the device that the manufacturer will need to submit either a Premarket Approval application or a 510(k) Premarket Notification. To have a clinical evaluation, an investigational plan must be approved by the institutional review board, the patients must have provided informed consent, the device must be labeled for investigational use only, the study must be monitored, and reports are required to be made.

Once a device is approved, the manufacturer must still comply with quality system regulations and good manufacturing practices. The regulations do not describe how a specific device must be manufactured but provide a framework that all manufacturers must follow for developing and following procedures. Manufacturers of medical devices must also annually register their establishment, or place of business, with the FDA. Once an establishment is registered, the manufacturer must provide the FDA with a list of the devices it manufactures.

The manufacturer must also abide by the FDA's labeling regulations, including requirements for the Directions for Use (DFU) that are typically provided to the doctor with the product and on the Internet. The DFU generally provides detailed product information, surgical techniques, a statement of risks and benefits, and a listing and description of common adverse events. Finally, if a device causes or contributes to the death or serious injury of an individual, it must be reported to the FDA under the Medical Device Reporting (MDR) program once the manufacturer learns of the death or serious injury. The goal of the MDR reporting program is to enable the FDA to timely detect and correct problems through data analysis.

Liability Theories

Although federal law defines and regulates medical devices, state law tort theories of liability and defenses are paramount to medical device products liability litigation. Consequently, the claims and defenses available in any particular matter will depend upon the state's law that is applied. While the law varies from state to state, the goal of products liability litigation does not. Medical device manufacturers, like manufacturers of any product, have a duty to "exercise ordinary and reasonable care not to expose the potential consumer to an unreasonable risk of harm from the use of its product."[4] Manufacturers are held liable for the products they create in order to protect the device's ultimate consumer from harm caused by the product. The common law and statutory schemes developed in the United States discourage manufacturers from producing products that will harm the public. They also hold the manufacturer responsible in the event that a product that is a menace to the public enters the marketplace.[5]

---

4. *See* Mack v. Stryker Corp., 748 F.3d 845, 849 (8th Cir. 2014).
5. *See* Tansy v. Dacomed Corp., 890 P.2d 881, 884 (Okla. 1994).

Design Defect

A design defect occurs when a medical device is defective or poses an unreasonable risk of danger even though the device meets the specifications of the manufacturer.[6] Design defects are inherent in the product. In other words, even though the product may serve the purpose it was intended for, the defect exists simply because the product was manufactured as specified by the manufacturer.

To prove a claim for a design defect, a plaintiff must typically prove that the product posed a substantial likelihood of harm as it was designed, that it was possible for the product to be designed in a safer manner, and that the defective design of the device was a substantial factor in causing the plaintiff's injury.[7]

The *Restatement (Second) of Torts* section 402A, which makes selling any product with a design defect a strict liability offense, applies in medical device cases. Section 402A provides that "one who sells any product in a defective condition unreasonably dangerous to the user or consumer or to his property is subject to liability for physical harm thereby caused to the ultimate user or consumer . . . if the seller is engaged in the business of selling the product and [the product] is expected to and does reach the user or consumer without substantial change in the condition in which it is sold."[8] According to the *Restatement*, this is the case even if the seller has taken all possible care in the preparation and sale of the product. California and many other states have found device manufacturers strictly liable for placing a product on the market that proves to have a defect and causes harm to an individual.[9] However, a device manufacturer is not an insurer or a guarantor of its product.[10] A plaintiff is still required to prove that the device was defective at the time it left the manufacturer's possession and that the condition was the cause, both in fact and proximately, of the plaintiff's injury.

Although tests vary by jurisdiction, a product is considered unreasonably dangerous due to its design when the product "fails to perform as safely as an ordinary customer would expect when used as intended or in a manner reasonably foreseeable by the manufacturer" or when the benefits of the device are outweighed by the risk of danger.[11] These tests are known as the consumer expectation test and the risk-utility test, respectively. The consumer expectation test is drawn from comment i to the *Restatement (Second) of Torts* section 402A. Comment i applies strict liability "only where the defective condition of the product makes it unreasonably dangerous to the user or consumer. . . . [T]he article sold must be dangerous to an extent beyond that which would be contemplated by the ordinary consumer who purchases it, with the ordinary knowledge common to the

6. Freeman v. Hoffman-La Roche, Inc., 618 N.W.2d 827, 833 (Neb. 2008).

7. Simon v. Smith & Nephew, 990 F. Supp. 2d 395, 403 (S.D.N.Y. 2013); *see also* Wolicki-Gables v. Arrow Int'l, Inc., 641 F. Supp. 2d 1270, 1285 (M.D. Fla. 2009).

8. Restatement (Second) of Torts § 402A (1965).

9. Tapia v. Davol, Inc., No. 15cv179-GPC (JLB), 2015 WL 4544507, at *5 (S.D. Cal. July 28, 2015).

10. Mack v. Stryker Corp., 748 F.3d 845, 850 (8th Cir. 2014); Fulton v. Pfizer Hosp. Prods. Grp., Inc., 872 S.W.2d 908, 912 (Tenn. Ct. App. 1993).

11. Wolicki-Gables v. Arrow Int'l, Inc., 641 F. Supp. 2d 1270, 1286 (M.D. Fla. 2009).

community as to its characteristics."[12] The consumer expectation test allows the jury to determine whether the product meets its expectations, rather than requiring expert testimony on the issue. For this reason, the consumer expectation test is best applied in cases where "the everyday experience of the product's users permits a conclusion that the product's design violated minimum safety assumptions, and is thus defective regardless of expert opinion about the merits of the design."[13] For this reason, the consumer expectation test is not often applied in medical device products liability litigation.[14]

Liability for a design defect can be established by arguing either that the risks of a medical device outweigh its benefit or that an alternative design exists.[15] The risk-utility test finds a product defective if the risks inherent in the device outweigh the utility or benefit derived from the product.[16] Factors considered in making the risk-utility analysis include

> the usefulness of the product; the gravity and severity of the danger posed by the design; the likelihood of that danger; the avoidability of the danger, i.e. the user's knowledge of the product, publicity surrounding the danger, or the efficacy of warnings, as well as common knowledge and expectation of danger, and the user's ability to avoid danger; the state of the art at the time the product is manufactured; the manufacturer's ability to eliminate the danger without impairing the product's usefulness or making it too expensive; and the feasibility of spreading the loss in the price or by purchasing insurance.[17]

The burden is on the plaintiff to prove that the risk of harm outweighs the utility of the design of the medical device.[18] "When the risk of harm outweighs the utility of a particular design, there is a determination that the manufacturer exposed the consumer to a greater risk of harm than is acceptable to society."[19]

Once it is shown that a medical device is defective, the plaintiff has to show general causation, that the device can cause the kind of injury the plaintiff suffered, and specific causation, that the device actually caused plaintiff's injuries.[20]

---

12. Restatement (Second) of Torts § 402A cmt. i (1965).

13. Morson v. Super. Ct., 90 Cal. App. 4th 775, 785 (Cal. Ct. App. 2001).

14. *See* Akkerman v. Metca Corp., 247 Fed. Appx. 895, 897–98 (9th Cir. 2007) ("Given that the medical world does not understand how ECT works—and that the ECT machine itself is a complicated device—a lay person would have no reasonable expectation as to how 'safe' the product should be.").

15. Mendez v. Shah, 28 F. Supp. 3d 282, 297 (D.N.J. 2014).

16. *In re* Mentor Corp. ObTape Transobturator Sling Prods. Liab. Litig., 711 F. Supp. 2d 1348, 1364 (M.D. Ga. 2010).

17. *Id.*

18. Cappellano v. Wright Med. Grp., Inc., 838 F. Supp. 2d 816, 827 (C.D. Ill. 2012).

19. *Id.*

20. *In re* Mentor, 711 F. Supp. 2d at 1365; *In re* Silicone Gel Breast Implants Prods. Liab. Litig., 318 F. Supp. 2d 879, 890 (C.D. Cal. 2004).

Manufacturing Defect

A medical device has been defectively manufactured when the individual medical device differs from the specifications and plans of the manufacturer.[21] Unlike a design defect, a manufacturing defect will often affect only a small portion of the total number of products produced. If the medical device that was used by the plaintiff is compared to the same product that was manufactured according to the manufacturing standards and fails to conform, it is a manufacturing defect.[22] Often, a manufacturing defect is the result of insufficient quality control.[23] When a party presents a claim for defective manufacturing, the premise of the claim is that the design of the product is suitable, but during the manufacturing process for the device at issue, the product was changed from its intended design.[24]

As with a design defect, a plaintiff must prove that the product suffered from a manufacturing defect and that the defect caused the plaintiff's injury.[25] To establish liability for a manufacturing defect, the defect must be a substantial factor in producing the injury.[26] Manufacturing defects can be demonstrated by either direct or circumstantial evidence.[27] Plaintiffs can prove a manufacturing defect exists through evidence of malfunction, evidence that eliminates abnormal use by the plaintiff, and evidence that "eliminate[s] reasonable secondary causes for the accident."[28]

Failure to Warn

A product that is properly designed and manufactured can still be found defective if the manufacturer does not include a proper warning with the product. Manufacturers are required to adequately warn consumers of a particular risk that "was known or knowable in light of the generally recognized and prevailing best scientific and medical knowledge available at the time of manufacture and distribution."[29] The existence and level of information required in a manufacturer's warning is dependent upon the foreseeability of the potential harm.[30]

---

21. Freeman v. Hoffman-La Roche, Inc., 618 N.W.2d 827, 833 (Neb. 2008); *see also* Tapia v. Davol, Inc., No. 15cv179-GPC (JLB), 2015 WL 4544507, at *5 (S.D. Cal. July 28, 2015).

22. Mendez v. Shah, 28 F. Supp. 3d 282, 298 (D.N.J. 2014).

23. Oja v. Howmedica, Inc., 111 F.3d 782, 792 (10th Cir. 1997).

24. *Mendez*, 28 F. Supp. 3d at 298.

25. Marmol v. St. Jude Med. Ctr., No. 8:15-cv-1276-T-30TGW, 2015 WL 5664890, at *5 (M.D. Fla. Sept. 24, 2015).

26. *Id.*

27. *Oja*, 111 F.3d at 792; Harrington v. Biomet, Inc., No. CIV-07-25-R, 2008 WL 2329132, at *3 (W.D. Okla. June 3, 2008).

28. Mracek v. Bryn Mawr Hosp., 610 F. Supp. 2d 401, 408 (E.D. Pa. 2009).

29. *Marmol*, No. 8:15-cv-1276-T-30TGW, at *8; Tapia v. Davol, Inc., No. 15cv179-GPC (JLB), 2015 WL 4544507, at *6 (S.D. Cal. July 28, 2015).

30. Mack v. Stryker Corp., 748 F.3d 845, 850 (8th Cir. 2014).

In medical device cases, the duty to warn is owed to the prescribing doctor, not the patient.[31] There is no duty to warn a doctor of a risk of which she already knew.[32] Additionally, if the risk is already known in the medical community, there is no need for a medical device manufacturer to provide a warning.[33] The warnings to the doctor must be adequate or reasonable under the circumstances of the case to find that the manufacturer properly warned the doctor.[34]

Causation can be an issue when trying to prove a claim for failure to warn, since doctors often will testify that they did not rely on the DFU provided with the medical device.[35] Doctors might also testify that they would not have changed their decision to use the medical device if they had received a better or more thorough warning.[36] Causation cannot be established in a failure to warn claim unless the plaintiff's physician actually read the warning or DFU that accompanied the product or relied on other statements made by the product's manufacturer.[37]

The duty to warn is a continuous one.[38] Manufacturers "must keep abreast of knowledge of their products as gained through research, adverse reaction reports, scientific literature and other available methods."[39] Once they obtain such knowledge, they must undertake to bring the knowledge to the attention of the medical profession.[40]

Breach of Express and Implied Warranties

In medical device litigation, claims based on breach of warranties are governed by the Uniform Commercial Code. Section 2-313 of the UCC governs express warranties and provides that a seller creates an express warranty when

> (a) an affirmation of fact or promise made by the seller to the buyer which relates to the goods and becomes part of the basis of the bargain creates an express warranty that the goods shall conform to the affirmation or promise.
>
> (b) any description of the goods which is made part of the basis of the bargain creates an express warranty that the goods shall conform to the description.

31. Huskey v. Ethicon, Inc., 29 F. Supp. 3d 736, 741 (S.D. W. Va. 2014).

32. *Id.*; *In re* Mentor ObTape Transobturator Sling Prods. Liab. Litig., 711 F. Supp. 2d 1348, 1366 (M.D. Ga. 2010) ("If the learned intermediary has actual knowledge of the substance of the alleged warning and would have taken the same course of action even with the information the plaintiff contends should have been provided then the plaintiff cannot establish causation.").

33. *Huskey*, 29 F. Supp. 3d at 741.

34. *In re Mentor*, 711 F. Supp. 2d at 1366.

35. *Id.*

36. *Huskey*, 29 F. Supp. 3d at 743.

37. *In re Mentor*, 711 F. Supp. 2d at 1378–79.

38. Rosen v. St. Jude Med., Inc., 41 F. Supp. 3d 170, 184 (N.D.N.Y. 2014).

39. *Id.*

40. *Id.*

(c) any sample or model which is made part of the basis of the bargain creates an express warranty that the whole of the goods shall conform to the sample or model.[41]

However, the seller can affirm the value of the good or provide a purchaser with his opinion regarding the product without creating a warranty.[42] Although some warranties require privity between the purchaser and the seller in order to create liability, no privity is required to bring a claim for breach of express warranty.[43]

To establish liability for breach of express warranty, the plaintiff must prove the exact terms of the warranty, that the plaintiff reasonably relied on the warranty, and that the breach of the warranty was a proximate cause of plaintiff's injury.[44] An example of the types of express warranties made by medical device manufacturers includes voluntary statements concerning approved uses or off-label uses.[45] In order to avoid preemption (discussed in more detail below), a breach of warranty claim must "identify specific representations of the manufacturer which exceeded the scope of the FDA approved statements, thereby establishing a contractual obligation voluntarily entered into by the manufacturer."[46]

A plaintiff in a warranty action does not have to prove that a defect exists; the failure of the device to perform as it was warranted is enough to prove breach of the express warranty.[47] However, the plaintiff is still required to prove causation.[48]

Medical device manufacturers can also be held liable for breach of the implied warranty of merchantability. The implied warrant of merchantability warrants that the goods sold will be fit for the ordinary purpose for which the particular goods are used.[49] This warranty "arises automatically in every sale of goods by one who is a merchant in those goods."[50] Implied warranties differ from express warranties because implied warranties arise from state law, whereas express warranties are created during the benefit of the bargain between the parties.[51] The focus of the inquiry is on the "expectations of the product's performance when used in the customary, usual, and reasonably foreseeable manner."[52] However, the goods are not required to fulfill every expectation of the buyer.[53] Plaintiffs will often have

41. U.C.C. § 2-313.
42. *Id.*
43. Tapia v. Davol, Inc., No. 15cv179-GPC (JLB), 2015 WL 4544507, at *7 (S.D. Cal. July 28, 2015).
44. *Id.*
45. Cornett v. Johnson & Johnson, 998 A.2d 543, 566 (N.J. Super. Ct. App. Div. 2010).
46. Horowitz v. Stryker Corp., 613 F. Supp. 2d 271, 285 (E.D.N.Y. 2009).
47. Mendez v. Shah, 28 F. Supp. 3d 282, 294 (D.N.J. 2014).
48. *Id.*
49. U.C.C. § 2-314.
50. Richman v. W.L. Gore & Assocs., Inc., 881 F. Supp. 895, 903 (S.D.N.Y. 1995).
51. *Id.* at 904.
52. Prohaska v. Sofamor, S.N.C., 138 F. Supp. 2d 422, 449 (W.D.N.Y. 2001).
53. *Id.*

to prove privity with the manufacturer to recover under this theory of liability.[54] A patient is typically not in privity with the manufacturer of a medical device, because the patient relies on the skill or judgment of her physician to provide a suitable product.[55]

Manufacturers also owe purchasers an implied warranty of fitness for a particular purpose. This warranty provides that if the seller is aware of the reason the device is being purchased while the parties are contracting, and the buyer relies on the seller's judgment in deciding to purchase the device, then the good is impliedly warranted to be fit for the use it was sold for.[56] A plaintiff therefore must allege "(1) the seller had reason to know of the particular purpose for which the buyer required the goods; (2) the buyer relied on the seller's skill and judgment to select suitable goods; and (3) the seller knew of the buyer's reliance on its skill and judgment."[57] Privity is typically required to bring a claim under this theory of liability.[58] As noted above, privity is difficult to prove in a medical device case because a patient most often relies on her physician's skill and judgment to select which medical device is appropriate for her, rather than depending on the manufacturer's judgment.[59] Some states have found that due to the nature of prescription medical devices, claims for implied warranty of fitness are barred.[60] They reach such a conclusion under the theory that, because medical devices are prescribed or selected for unique individuals by their individual physicians, medical devices do not have "an ordinary purpose," and claims of breach of implied warranty of fitness must therefore fail.[61]

A defendant can disclaim its warranties under some circumstances.[62] An implied warranty of merchantability can be disclaimed if the disclaimer includes the word "merchantability" and is conspicuous.[63] A warranty of fitness can be disclaimed if the disclaimer is in writing and is conspicuous.[64] A term is conspicuous if it is written such that a reasonable person who might have raised the implied warranty should have noticed it.[65] As long as a disclaimer is conspicuous, the

54. Tapia v. Davol, Inc., No. 15cv179-GPC (JLB), 2015 WL 4544507, at *8 (S.D. Cal. July 28, 2015); *In re* Mentor ObTape Transobturator Sling Prods. Liab. Litig., 711 F. Supp. 2d 1348, 1366 (M.D. Ga. 2010).

55. *Tapia*, 2015 WL 4544507, at *8; Gowen v. Cady, 376 S.E.2d 390, 393 (Ga. Ct. App. 1988).

56. U.C.C. § 2-315.

57. Gerk v. CL Med. Sarl, MDL No. 15-1145, 2015 WL 7002802, at *2 (C.D. Ill. Nov. 10, 2015).

58. *Tapia*, 2015 WL 4544507, at *8.

59. Evraets v. Intermedics Intraocular, Inc., 34 Cal. Rptr. 2d 852, 857 (Ct. App. 1994).

60. Davenport v. Medtronic, Inc., 302 F. Supp. 2d 419, 441 (E.D. Pa. 2004).

61. Cogswell v. Wright Med. Tech., Inc., No. 15-295, 2015 WL 4393385, at *5 (W.D. Pa. July 16, 2015).

62. *See* Scanion v. Medtronic Sofamore Danek USA Inc., 61 F. Supp. 3d 403, 413 (D. Del. 2014).

63. Bruce v. ICI Ams., Inc., 933 F. Supp. 781, 790–91 (S.D. Iowa 1996).

64. *Id.* at 791.

65. *Id.*

purchaser does not even have to read the disclaimer to disclaim the warranty as long as the consumer has a reasonable opportunity to read it.[66]

Fraud/Misrepresentation

To bring a claim for negligent misrepresentation, a plaintiff must show that a misrepresentation was made to him about an existing material fact, the person who made the misrepresentation did so without having a reasonable ground for believing it to be true, the person making the misrepresentation did so with the intent to induce the plaintiff's reliance on the fact misrepresented, the plaintiff justifiably relied on the misrepresentation, and the plaintiff suffered damage as a result of the misrepresentation.[67]

Plaintiffs can also allege fraudulent misrepresentation against the manufacturers of medical devices. The elements of fraudulent misrepresentation include a representation to the plaintiff by the defendant that an important fact is true, the representation was false, the defendant knew that the representation was false when he made it or the defendant acted recklessly in making the representation, the defendant intended that the plaintiff rely on the representation, the plaintiff reasonably relied on the representation, the plaintiff suffered a harm, and the plaintiff's reliance on the representation was a substantial factor in causing the plaintiff's harm.[68] As is required with any other claim for fraud, a plaintiff must plead her claim with particularity.

Fraud and misrepresentation claims usually arise in the context of the manufacturer's advertising and marketing campaigns for a medical device.[69]

Plaintiffs will sometimes allege that the manufacturer misled the FDA about the safety or effectiveness of a device in order to secure permission to market the device. However, such a claim for "fraud on the FDA" is not actionable. In *Buckman Co. v. Plaintiffs' Legal Committee*, the Supreme Court held that the FDCA preempted state law causes of action that sought to supplant the FDA's role in policing fraud on the agency, which was a power Congress exclusively granted to it in the FDCA.[70] The Court also noted that the "FDCA leaves no doubt that it is the federal government rather than private litigants who are authorized to file suit for noncompliance" with its provisions.[71] Many circuits have held that claims based

---

66. *Id.*

67. Tapia v. Davol, Inc., No. 15cv179-GPC (JLB), 2015 WL 4544507, at *13 (S.D. Cal. July 28, 2015); *see also* Gerk v. CL Med. Sarl, No. 15-1145, 2015 WL 7002802, at *3 (C.D. Ill. Nov. 10, 2015).

68. *Tapia*, 2015 WL 4544507, at *13; Arthur v. Medtronic, Inc., No. 4:14-cv-52 (CEJ), 2015 WL 5012312, at *2 (E.D. Mo. Aug. 24, 2015).

69. Mendez v. Shah, 28 F. Supp. 3d 282, 301 (D.N.J. 2014); Alton v. Medtronic, Inc., 970 F. Supp. 2d 1069, 1097–98 (D. Or. 2013); Gerk v. CL Med. Sarl, No. 15-1145, 2015 WL 7002802, at *4 (C.D. Ill. Nov. 10, 2015) (plaintiff alleged that the manufacturer knew its product was defective, plaintiff's doctor relied on the manufacturer's claims with regard to the product, and the manufacturer had attempted to conceal information related to the safety of the medical device).

70. Buckman Co. v. Plaintiffs' Legal Comm., 531 U.S. 341, 350 (2001).

71. *Id.* at 349 n.4.

on an allegation that the manufacturer defrauded the FDA are preempted under the *Buckman* ruling.[72] This is because allowing actions based on such allegations would effectively "allow individual juries to undertake a counterfactual review, and conclude the FDA would not approve the device."[73]

Occasionally, plaintiffs will sue the manufacturer's sales representative for fraud or misrepresentation in an attempt to avoid federal jurisdiction based on diversity of citizenship. Defendant manufacturers sometimes remove anyway, arguing the doctrine of fraudulent joinder. Under this doctrine, "in a suit with named defendants who are not of diverse citizenship from the plaintiff, the diverse defendant may still remove the action if it can establish that the non-diverse defendants were fraudulently named or joined solely to defeat diversity jurisdiction."[74] To prove that the defendant was fraudulently joined, the defendant seeking removal must demonstrate that there is no reasonable basis to support a claim against the joined defendant or no real good-faith intention to litigate the claim against the joined defendant.[75] This is a very heavy burden for the defendant. For example, in *Hricik v. Stryker Biotech, LLC*, the Eastern District of Pennsylvania stated that "regardless of whether individual sales representatives have a duty to warn the physicians to whom they promote medical devices about the risks associated with the devices, there is a colorable basis for a claim that the sales representatives have a duty to refrain from affirmatively misrepresenting the safety and efficacy of devices for uses for which they have not been approved."[76]

In some cases, the plaintiff will allege that the sales representatives made misrepresentations to doctors while in the operating room with regard to off-label uses of the medical device.[77] Defendants can defend against these claims by arguing that doctors still maintain an independent duty to ensure they are making proper medical decisions and therefore the causation element cannot be established. Allegations of misrepresentation arising from a medical sales representative stating that a product is appropriate for a particular patient will not likely support a claim for misrepresentation because "whether a particular medical device or procedure is appropriate for a specific patient is particularly dependent upon the patient's medical history and condition, factors that are not within the purview of a sales representative's expertise."[78] Further, statements of opinion cannot support liability for a fraud claim.[79]

---

72. *See* Cooper v. Smith & Nephew, Inc., 259 F.3d 194, 203 n.3 (4th Cir. 2001).

73. Kemp v. Medtronic Inc., 231 F.3d 216, 235–36 (6th Cir. 2000); *see also* Hughes v. Cook, 452 F. Supp. 2d 832, 842 (W.D. Tenn. 2006) (finding plaintiff's Tennessee tort claims preempted).

74. Hricik v. Stryker Biotech, LLC, 89 F. Supp. 3d 694, 700 (E.D. Pa. 2015).

75. *Id.*

76. *Id.* at 704.

77. Hawkins v. Medtronic, Inc., 62 F. Supp. 3d 1144 (E.D. Cal. 2014).

78. Arthur v. Medtronic, Inc., No. 4:14-cv-52 (CEJ), 2015 WL 5012312, at *3 (E.D. Mo. Aug. 25, 2015).

79. *Id.*

Defenses

Causation

Failure to prove medical causation will defeat a products liability case involving a medical device.[80] It is plaintiff's burden to prove both general and specific causation with regard to the medical device. To establish causation, the plaintiff has to prove that his injury was caused by reason of a defect built into the medical device that existed at the time of his injury.[81] A plaintiff will need expert medical testimony "where injuries are of a character requiring skilled and professional [persons] to determine the cause and extent."[82] A plaintiff must show that the defect was both the cause in fact and the legal cause of his injuries.[83] There are two tests that are often used to determine whether an action is the cause in fact of an injury: the "substantial factor" test and the "but for" test.[84] The "substantial factor" test asks whether the defendant's conduct "is a material element and a substantial factor in bringing about the plaintiff's injury."[85] The "but for" test asks whether the injury would have occurred without the defendant's conduct. If the injury would have still occurred, the defendant's conduct is not the cause in fact of the injury.[86] Ultimately, causation does not exist where the injuries are too remote, indirect, or purely coincidental.[87]

If the determination of whether the injury was caused by some conduct is "presumed not to be within the common knowledge and experience, competent medical opinion is necessary to enable a jury to find the requisite causation."[88] "To prove proximate causation for medical conditions or illnesses allegedly caused by a defective product, a plaintiff must show by a reasonable degree of medical certainty that the disease or injury was caused by the defective product."[89] One of the standard ways an expert analyzes causation in a medical device case is to perform a differential diagnosis. A differential diagnosis "is a standard scientific technique of identifying the cause of a medical problem by eliminating the likely causes until the more probable one is isolated."[90] Differential diagnosis can be used only to

80. Alexander v. Smith & Nephew, P.L.C., 90 F. Supp. 2d 1225, 1232 (N.D. Okla. 2000); *see also* Hart well v. Danek Med., Inc., 47 F. Supp. 2d 703, 707 (W.D. Va. 1999) ("To succeed on a products liability claim, the plaintiff must demonstrate that a product defect is the only reasonable explanation or cause of the complained-of injury.").

81. *Alexander*, 90 F. Supp. 2d at 1232.

82. *Id.*

83. Huskey v. Ethicon, Inc., 29 F. Supp. 3d 736, 742 (S.D. W. Va. 2014).

84. *Id.*

85. *Id.*

86. *Id.*

87. Rosen v. St. Jude Med., Inc., 41 F. Supp. 3d 170, 187 (N.D.N.Y. 2014).

88. Prohaska v. Sofamor, S.N.C., 138 F. Supp. 2d 422, 435 (W.D.N.Y. 2001).

89. Botnick v. Zimmer, Inc., 484 F. Supp. 2d 715, 724 (N.D. Ohio 2007).

90. *Prohaska*, 138 F. Supp. 2d at 438.

demonstrate specific causation, as general causation is an assumption made in the differential diagnosis before any other possible causes can be eliminated.[91]

Alternative causation is one key way to defend a claim in medical device products liability litigation. Typically, patients that are undergoing a surgery where a medical device is going to be implanted will suffer from any number of other conditions. Depending on the facts of the case, it may be possible to defeat causation by having an expert demonstrate that the injury the plaintiff is complaining of was actually caused by a preexisting condition.[92]

Federal Preemption

In every medical device case, the practitioner must evaluate whether the plaintiff's state law tort claims can survive the defense of federal preemption. That is because the Medical Device Amendment to the Food, Drug, and Cosmetics Act contains an express preemption provision that states:

> No state or political subdivision of a State may establish or continue in effect with respect to a device intended for human use any requirement (1) which is different from, or in addition to, any requirement applicable under this chapter to the device, and (2) which relates to the safety or effectiveness of the device or to any other matter included in a requirement applicable to the device under this chapter.[93]

While the topic of federal preemption is beyond the scope of this chapter, it is important to recognize that the Supreme Court has held that preemption under the express provision will be applied when "the federal government established requirements applicable to the medical device in question, and the state-law claims concerning the device are based on requirements that are different from, or in addition to, the federal requirements and relate to the safety and effectiveness of the device."[94] As a result, devices that receive the FDA's approval under the Premarket Approval process, but not devices that were cleared by the FDA under the 510(k) process, are entitled to federal preemption.[95] Still, express federal preemption disposes of numerous cases based on state law tort claims and must be carefully considered in every medical device case.

The MDA also has an implied preemption provision that requires that any action seeking to enforce or penalize violations of the FDCA be brought by the United States.[96] The space left for civil plaintiffs to sue for defective design of a product that is approved by the FDA is limited. Essentially, a plaintiff "must be

---

91. *In re* Breast Implant Litig., 11 F. Supp. 2d 1217, 1230 (D. Colo. 1998).

92. *See Prohaska*, 138 F. Supp. 2d at 439.

93. 21 U.S.C. § 360k(a).

94. Riegel v. Medtronic, Inc., 552 U.S. 312, 321–22 (2008).

95. Medtronic v. Lohr, 518 U.S. 480, 492 (1996); Lewis v. Johnson & Johnson, 991 F. Supp. 2d 748, 752 (S.D. W. Va. 2014).

96. 21 U.S.C. § 337(a).

suing for conduct that violates the FDCA (or else his claim is expressly preempted by 360k), but the plaintiff must not be suing because the conduct violates the FDCA (such claim would be impliedly preempted under *Buckman*)."[97]

The Learned Intermediary Doctrine

The learned intermediary doctrine is applied in failure to warn cases where "a physician is the intermediary between a defendant pharmaceutical . . . manufacturer and an injured patient."[98] Under this doctrine, a pharmaceutical manufacturer discharges its duty to warn the individual patient by providing adequate warnings to the physician.[99] This doctrine is grounded in the belief that physicians "are in a better position to assess the risks and determine when a particular patient reasonably should be informed about a risk."[100] When a doctor who has been adequately informed of the risks by a product manufacturer fails to warn an individual patient, her "quarrel is with the doctor rather than the drug manufacturer."[101]

The learned intermediary doctrine changes who must receive a manufacturer's warning and how the adequacy of the warning should be judged.[102] In a typical products liability case, the warning must be given to the end user. However, in a medical device products liability case, the warning must be given to the doctor instead of the patient. The doctor serves as the gatekeeper between the patient and the manufacturer.[103] Therefore, the manufacturer owes a duty to warn the doctor, and the doctor has the duty of ultimately warning the patient.[104] The doctor has to consider the best fit for the patient when selecting the medical device and also has to select which warnings to pass along to the patient.[105]

This doctrine allows a medical device manufacturer to "reasonably rely on intermediaries to transmit their warnings and instructions."[106] Doctors are typically in a better position to know what kind of medical device a patient needs than the patient would be himself. Further, patients are expected to rely on the judgment of the doctor.[107]

To recover under the learned intermediary doctrine, a plaintiff must prove that a manufacturer failed to warn the doctor of a risk associated with the device that

97. *In re* Medtronic Inc., Sprint Fidelis Leads Prods. Liab. Litig., 623 F.3d 1200, 1204 (8th Cir. 2010).

98. Payne v. Novartis Pharm. Corp., 767 F.3d 526, 530 (6th Cir. 2014).

99. *Id.* at 531.

100. Laws v. Johnson, 799 S.W.2d 249, 254 (Tenn. Ct. App. 1990).

101. *Payne*, 767 F.3d at 531.

102. Hurley v. Heart Physicians, P.C., 278 Conn. 305, 317 n.10 (2006); McCombs v. Synthes (U.S.A.), 587 S.E.2d 594, 595 (Ga. 2003); Tyree v. Bos. Scientific Corp., 56 F. Supp. 3d 826, 833 (S.D. W. Va. 2014).

103. *McCombs*, 587 S.E.2d at 595.

104. O'Connell v. Biomet, Inc., 250 P.3d 1278, 1281–82 (Colo. App. 2010).

105. Huskey v. Ethicon, Inc., 29 F. Supp. 3d 736, 743 (S.D. W. Va. 2014).

106. Pittman v. Upjohn Co., 890 S.W.2d 425, 429 (Tenn. 1994).

107. Alexander v. Smith & Nephew, P.L.C., 90 F. Supp. 2d 1225, 1235 (N.D. Okla. 2000).

was unknown to the doctor and that failure was the cause in fact and the proximate cause of the plaintiff's injury.[108] This is a large burden for a plaintiff to bear, as the plaintiff must prove that his doctor would have acted differently if he was provided with more expansive warnings.[109] This is difficult to prove because "medical ethics as well as medical practice dictate independent medical judgment, unaffected by the manufacturer's control, on the part of the doctor."[110]

Medical Device Litigation Is Generally Not Suitable for Class Action Lawsuits

Federal Rule of Civil Procedure 23 provides the requirements for bringing a class action lawsuit.[111] The requirements include commonality, typicality, adequacy of representation, and numerosity.[112] Given the vastly different injuries and issues with causation in a medical device products liability litigation, courts have struggled to find class certification appropriate.

Because there is no true common cause of the injury plaintiffs suffer in medical device products liability litigation, the facts and the legal issues must be developed on a case-by-case basis.[113] For example, the Sixth Circuit in *In re American Medical Systems, Inc.* stated that "proofs as to strict liability, negligence, failure to warn, breach of express and implied warranties will also vary from plaintiff to plaintiff because complications with an AMS device may be due to a variety of factors, including surgical error, improper use of the device, anatomical incompatibility, infection, device malfunction, or psychological problems."[114] Additionally, in medical device products liability cases, the individual prescribing doctors must testify to determine issues with warnings, causations, and damages.[115] The same is true of the affirmative defenses the defendant raises.[116]

Because "the products are different, each plaintiff has a unique complaint, and each receives different information and assurances from his treating physician," the economies of scale that would be achieved by proceeding as a class action are greatly diminished by the individualization of the issues.[117] Courts, then, will use multidistrict litigation to increase the efficiency of the legal system when a number of suits are brought against the same manufacturer because class actions are

---

108. Harden v. Danek Med., Inc., 985 S.W.2d 449, 451–52 (Tenn. Ct. App. 1998).
109. Sanchez v. Bos. Scientific Corps., 38 F. Supp. 3d 727, 732 (S.D. W. Va. 2014).
110. *Id.* at 733.
111. Fed. R. Civ. P. 23.
112. *Id.*
113. *In re* Am. Med. Sys., Inc., 75 F.3d 1069, 1084 (6th Cir. 1996); *see also* Raye v. Medtronic Corp., 696 F. Supp. 1273, 1275 (D. Minn. 1988).
114. *In re* Am. Med. Sys., Inc., 75 F.3d at 1081.
115. *Id.*
116. *Id.* at 1085.
117. *Id.*

typically unworkable.[118] Cases involving design defects will often be litigated in multidistrict litigation, because the alleged defect will exist in all of the products produced.

Unavoidably Unsafe Products

Comment k to the *Restatement (Second) of Torts* section 402A excludes certain products from strict liability, stating:

> There are some products, which in the present state of human knowledge, are quite incapable of being made safe for their intended and ordinary use. These are especially common in the field of drugs. . . . Such a product, properly prepared, and accompanied by proper directions and warnings, is not defective, nor is it unreasonably dangerous.[119]

Although comment k was initially applied solely to prescription drug cases, a number of courts have now extended the protections of comment k to medical device manufacturers.[120] Public policy supports this extension because medical devices, like prescription drugs, are often unreasonably dangerous but offer great benefit to society.[121] Comment k attempts to balance a manufacturer's responsibility to develop and market safe products with the need to develop new products.[122] "It protects certain manufacturers who develop new products which at the time of manufacture are incapable of being made totally safe, and shields certain products by classifying them as unavoidably unsafe rather than defective."[123]

This defense is only available when the medical device is properly manufactured and contains adequate warnings.[124] Additionally, the medical device must be as safe as it can be using the best testing and research available at the time of manufacture. To support this affirmative defense, a manufacturer must show that "the device was incapable of being made safe; properly prepared and marketed; and accompanied by a proper warning."[125]

---

118. *See* Sanchez v. Bos. Scientific Corp., 38 F. Supp. 3d 727 (S.D. W. Va. 2014) (case was one of more than 60,000 assigned to judge in multidistrict litigation).

119. Restatement (Second) of Torts § 402A cmt. k; *see* Wilson v. Synthes USA Prods., LLC, No. 14-4724, 2015 WL 4378576, at *2 (E.D. Pa. July 16, 2015).

120. *Wilson*, 2015 WL 4378576, at *2; Harwell v. Am. Med. Sys., Inc., 803 F. Supp. 1287 (M.D. Tenn. 1992); Hufft v. Horowitz, 4 Cal. App. 4th 8 (Dist. Ct. App. 1992); Perfetti v. McGhan, 662 P.2d 646 (N.M. Ct. App. 1983).

121. *Wilson*, 2015 WL 4378576, at *3; *see also* Prather v. Abbott Labs., 960 F. Supp. 2d 700, 707 (W.D. Ky. 2013).

122. Tansy v. Dacomed Corp., 890 P.2d 881, 884 (Okla. 1994).

123. *Id.* at 885.

124. *Id.* at 886.

125. Byrnes v. Small, 60 F. Supp. 3d 1289, 1299 (M.D. Fla. 2015).

Damages

Compensatory Damages

The purpose of compensatory damages is to compensate a plaintiff for the harm caused by the defendant's product.[126] The goal of this category of damages is to put the plaintiff in the same condition she was in before the injury occurred. Compensatory damages cover both economic and noneconomic loss. Economic loss includes things like medical expenses, the cost of any disability or permanent injury, and lost profits or wages. Noneconomic damages compensate plaintiffs for aspects of their injury that are not easily quantifiable, such as pain and suffering.

A number of states apply the economic loss doctrine in products liability cases, thereby prohibiting a plaintiff from suing under tort theories for economic losses with respect to damage to the product itself and consequential damages resulting from the alleged defect. The rationale of the doctrine is that in such cases, contract principles are more appropriate than tort principles for resolving economic losses.[127] However, the economic loss doctrine does not apply to prohibit recovery when the product defect led to personal injury and/or economic losses beyond the damage to the device itself.[128]

Punitive Damages

Punitive damages serve a different purpose than compensatory damages; they are awarded to plaintiffs to punish defendants for particularly egregious behavior. They also serve to deter other manufacturers from acting like the defendant.[129] It is rare, but not unheard of, for punitive damages to be awarded in a medical device case. In most instances, the court will award punitive damages only when the conduct undertaken by the defendant is malicious, reckless, or oppressive.[130] "Punitive damages, the purpose of which is to 'punish, penalize or deter,' are, as a general rule, improper where a defendant has adhered to the relevant safety regulations."[131] However, regulatory compliance will not defeat an award of punitive damages where there is evidence that demonstrates culpable behavior on the part of the manufacturer.[132] A court may award punitive damages when a manufacturer has knowledge of a particular risk but fails to warn of or address the known risk or when the manufacturer conceals that the material used in the product was prohibited from being implanted in the human body.[133] In *In re C.R. Bard, Inc.*, the court

126. McDarby v. Merck & Co., Inc., 949 A.2d 223, 274 (N.J. 2008).
127. Gill-Samuel v. Nova Biomed. Corp., 298 F.R.D. 693, 696 (S.D. Fla. 2014).
128. *Id.* at 697.
129. Sanchez v. Bos. Scientific Corp., 38 F. Supp. 3d 727, 738–39 (S.D. W. Va. 2014).
130. *See* Kee v. Zimmer, Inc., 871 F. Supp. 2d 405, 413 (E.D. Pa. 2012).
131. Edwards v. Ethicon, Inc., 30 F. Supp. 3d 554, 564 (S.D. W. Va. 2014).
132. *Id.*
133. *In re* C.R. Bard, Inc., No. 2187, 2013 WL 2432871, at *4–10 (S.D. W. Va. June 4, 2013).

found that the plaintiff put forth sufficient evidence to avoid summary judgment on the issue of punitive damages when she demonstrated that Bard had the Material Safety Data Sheet, which prohibited the use of the material for implant in a human. The plaintiff also demonstrated that Bard concealed from the manufacturer of a component part that the resulting product was going to be implanted in a human. Finally, the plaintiff demonstrated that Bard conducted animal testing that failed to support the safety of the product and marketed the medical device anyway.[134] Other courts will consider the marketing schemes of manufacturers and use false claims of safety to support an award for punitive damages.[135] Such actions essentially demonstrate a conscious disregard of the safety of the end user of the medical device and therefore warrant an award of punitive damages.

In contrast, some states have expressly disallowed punitive damages in their products liability statutes when the products have been approved or generally recognized as safe by the FDA.[136] Others have enacted statutes that require plaintiffs to prove that the defendant is guilty of oppression, fraud, or malice by clear and convincing evidence.[137]

Conclusion

This chapter has discussed liability theories, defenses, and damages common to medical device cases. The brief overview of the federal regulation of medical devices demonstrated the unique position of medical devices in the federal regulatory system as well as in the marketplace, making litigation involving medical devices generally more complex. This chapter then explored the state law tort theories of liability that are paramount to medical device products liability litigation, as well as defenses that have been effective in defeating liability. Finally, this chapter explored the various types of damages a plaintiff may seek in medical device products liability litigation. Although this chapter sought to provide a basic understanding of medical device litigation generally, jurisdiction-specific research should still be undertaken before involvement in any medical device products liability litigation.

134. *Id.* at *9–10; *see also* Hillard v. A.H. Robins Co., 148 Cal. App. 3d 374, 397 (Ct. App. 1983) (finding trial court erred in directing verdict for defendant on issue of punitive damages where evidence showed that employees reported risks to manufacturer and manufacturer continued to market the device without any changes).

135. Palmer v. A.H. Robins Co., 684 P.2d 187, 220–21 (Colo. 1984).

136. *See* Ariz. Rev. Stat. § 12-689.

137. Cal. Civ. Code § 3294(a); *see also* Sanchez v. Bos. Scientific Corp., 38 F. Supp. 3d 727, 743 (S.D. W. Va. 2014) ("A reasonable jury could find that by ignoring a warning on the MSDS and failing to conduct clinical testing, BSC's actions were 'despicable conduct' with willful and conscious disregard of the safety of consumers.").

5

STATUTES OF LIMITATION, TOLLING, TORT DAMAGE CAPS, CERTIFICATES OF MEDICAL MERIT, AND VENUE

James Bush

This chapter is, in large part, a survey of a landscape shaped by states' medical tort reform efforts. Tort reform is an intensely political topic, and statutes of limitation, tolling, damage caps, certificates of merit, and venue are just some of the means used to regulate what has been alternatively described as a real or merely perceived "lawsuit crisis" in the volume and impact of medical tort claims.[1] While the substance of that debate is not addressed here, the effect has been the creation of a legal terrain that varies significantly among states and is frequently reshaped by the political process and litigation.

Especially in light of this constantly and quickly changing landscape, all practitioners, whether experienced in or new to medical tort litigation, should tread with a keen eye to detail, become familiar with the basic public policy considerations at play, vigilantly update research, keep abreast of political developments and appellate litigation, and regularly confer with colleagues practicing in the area. Doing so will allow for effective early case assessment.

Statutes of Limitation: Language Is Key

Statutes of limitation are the chief means employed by state legislatures to curtail the volume of various lawsuits, and medical tort claims receive particular attention. Limitations for medical tort claims are almost always distinct from common negligence claims and are often shorter in their periods of both limitation and repose. Many limitation statutes also contain specialized provisions for the unique ways in which medical tort claims accrue, including a "discovery rule," tolling in instances of claims by minors or those with disabilities, tolling in instances of fraud or intentional concealment, and tolling for claims relating to the discovery

1. F. Patrick Hubbard, *The Nature and Impact of the "Tort Reform" Movement*, 35 Hofstra L. Rev. 437, 469–71 (2006).

of foreign bodies. Further, many statutes also contain procedural tolling periods intended to encourage presuit investigation and early resolution without the need for costly litigation.[2]

All litigators know the importance of determining the applicable limitation period at the very outset of a claim. While medical tort claims are no different, they do require an informed and meticulous approach. On receiving the claim, a practitioner should first identify all appropriate limitation provisions. This process is often complex with medical tort claims due to the number of separate provisions that may apply. For instance, a medical tort claim might encompass malpractice, wrongful death, survival, and consortium claims, each of which is frequently addressed in a separate chapter or section. States' medical tort limitation statutes may be contained within more generic limitation statutes addressing a variety of civil claims.[3] They may exist within a statutory scheme addressing medical torts exclusively.[4] Alternatively, as is usually the case, applicable provisions will be fragmented across a variety of chapters or sections simultaneously, as in New York,[5] Florida,[6] and Michigan.[7]

Beyond statutory language, states may also address the operation of the medical tort limitation period within their civil rules of procedure.[8] Accordingly, practitioners should closely review both a state's statutes and rules of procedure to identify all applicable limitation provisions.

Next, a careful reading of the language is needed to determine applicability to the claim. In medical tort claims, statutory definitions are critical, and practitioners should pay special attention to any definition sections provided within the relevant section or chapter. Often, unique terms of art exist for who qualifies as a "healthcare provider,"[9] what constitutes "care,"[10] and which "claim(s)" are subject to the limitation period.[11] Language that would appear to have plain meaning may have a less than intuitive and even arbitrary application in practice. For instance, in Florida, the term "healthcare provider" includes a list of 25 different individual professionals and entities but, notably, the term excludes nursing homes[12] and

2. *See, e.g.*, FLA. STAT. ANN. § 766.201(1)(c).
3. *E.g.*, IDAHO CODE ANN. § 5-219(4).
4. *E.g.*, TEX. CIV. PRAC. & REM. CODE § 74.251.
5. N.Y. C.P.L.R. §§ 208, 214-a.
6. Florida enacted distinct statutes of limitation for three types of medical tort claims. One exists for claims of medical malpractice. FLA. STAT. ANN. § 95.11(4)(b). A second exists for nursing home malpractice. FLA. STAT. ANN. § 400.0236. A third exists for claims against assisted living facilities. FLA. STAT. ANN. § 429.296.
7. MICH. COMP. LAWS ANN. §§ 600.5805(6), 600.5838a.
8. FLA. R. CIV. P. 1.650(d).
9. *E.g.*, FLA. STAT. ANN. § 766.202(4); TEX. CIV. PRAC. & REM. CODE § 74.001(8), (11), (12); WASH. REV. CODE § 7.70.020.
10. *E.g.*, TEX. CIV. PRAC. & REM. CODE § 74.001(7), (10).
11. *E.g.*, CAL. CIV. PROC. CODE § 340.5(1); FLA. STAT. ANN. § 95.11(4)(b); 735 ILL. COMP. STAT. ANN. 5/13-212(a); TEX. CIV. PRAC. & REM. CODE § 74.001(13).
12. FLA. STAT. ANN. § 400.0236; Benjamin v. Tandem Healthcare Inc., 998 So. 2d 566 (Fla. 2008).

assisted living facilities.[13] These entities have their own limitation statutes with shorter periods of repose than other medical malpractice actions.[14] This is a detail that could easily be overlooked were one unwittingly and perhaps understandably to assume nursing homes and assisted living facilities were "healthcare providers."

Further, some limitation statutes, such as New York's, may spotlight medical tort claims and deal with them specifically while excluding other theories of recovery.[15] Others may operate more inclusively, as in Illinois, where the limitations statute includes actions "whether based upon tort, or breach of contract, or otherwise, arising out of patient care."[16] Thus, terms of art regarding facts, parties, and claims merit special focus.

Once the applicable limitation provisions are identified and any definitions parsed, practitioners will note that all statutes provide an initial period of limitation, which is often shorter than claims for ordinary negligence. This period can vary significantly depending on jurisdiction. Some states, such as California, Ohio, Kentucky, Louisiana, and Tennessee, have limitation periods that can operate to provide only *one year* in which to file medical tort claims.[17] The majority of states, however, observe basic limitation periods ranging from two years[18] to three years.[19]

Of course, the first step in calculating the limitation period depends on the date of accrual. Similar to other tort claims, medical tort limitation statutes have a basic date of injury provision—a simple matter when all elements of the cause of action are readily identifiable and occur at or near the same time. The classic scenario is a wrong site surgery, in which a procedure is done to the wrong side or site of the body, the wrong procedure is performed, or the wrong patient receives the procedure. Conceivably, the injury and its discovery happen at or near the same time and accrual is clear.

In practice, however, medical tort claims often accrue on initially murky timelines. In a basic example, a physician may, unbeknownst to her patient, fail to properly diagnose a treatable cancer in year one. In year two, the patient begins to exhibit symptoms that could be consistent with cancer, but he fails to seek treatment immediately. Months later, in routine diagnostic testing, the patient fortuitously discovers the cancer, which is now inoperable. Thus, in addition to basic "date of injury" provisions for accrual, these statutes often provide for a discovery

---

13. FLA. STAT. ANN. § 449.296.

14. The statute of repose for medical malpractice actions against "healthcare providers" is seven years. FLA. STAT. ANN. § 96.11(4)(b). However, for nursing homes and assisted living facilities, it is six years. FLA. STAT. ANN. §§ 449.296, 400.0236. The difference illustrates the effect of separate tort reform battles in the state legislature.

15. N.Y. C.P.L.R. §§ 208, 214-a.

16. 735 ILL. COMP. STAT. ANN. 5/13-212(a).

17. CAL. CIV. PROC. CODE § 340.5; KY. REV. STAT. ANN. §§ 413.140, 413.170; LA. REV. STAT. ANN. § 9:5628; OHIO REV. CODE ANN. § 2305.113(A); TENN. CODE ANN. §§ 29-26-116, 28-1-106.

18. *E.g.*, FLA. STAT. ANN. § 95.11(4)(b); 735 ILL. COMP. STAT. ANN. 5/13-212(a); TEX. CIV. PRAC. & REM. CODE § 74.251.

19. *E.g.*, ME. REV. STAT. ANN. tit. 24, § 2902; MASS. GEN. LAWS ANN. ch. 260, § 4.

rule that can adjust the date of accrual to when an injury is, or should be, discovered by a claimant with due diligence.

Discovery rules typically function in one of two ways and, depending on the state, they do not always benefit the claimant. In one iteration, the upper time limit on the initial limitation period is set, and later discovery of the injury can only serve to extend that time further, such as in Mississippi.[20] On the other hand, a general limitation period may be specified, but earlier discovery of the injury can serve to shorten that time period, such as in California.[21]

Issues of accrual can be highly fact dependent and are hotly litigated. They require practitioners to understand not only the limitation language but also the medical issues at play. Consulting with a qualified medical expert is almost always a critical component of early case assessment. Nonspecific signs and symptoms of disease or injury can easily cloud the accrual timeline. Patients' medical status can also hamper their ability to diligently detect problems. Qualified medical experts should be able to assist the practitioner by precisely explaining how and when breaches in the standard of care occurred and what options existed for timely diagnosis and treatment under the circumstances. For more information on experts, see Chapter 8.

Statutes of Limitation: Tolling and Repose

For medical torts, many states set out special provisions for tolling the initial limitation period, which, predictably, can vary widely in their operation and ultimate duration. Tolling periods may exist for many scenarios, including claims by minors and persons with disabilities, as well as those concerning foreign bodies or instances of fraud or intentional concealment. Additionally, many states provide more routine procedural tolling periods meant to foster presuit resolution of medical tort claims.

The most common tolling provision in medical tort limitation statutes is for claims by minors. These often operate in addition to discovery rules to extend the basic limitation period, providing a short period of extra time for a minor to file a claim. There is a spectrum of approaches, and tolling provisions for minors do not necessarily apply to all persons under age 18. For example, in Alabama, an injured party under age four has until his eighth birthday to commence a medical tort action.[22] Alabama provides no other special treatment for minors. Likewise, in Texas, minors under age 12 have until their 14th birthday to file a medical tort claim; otherwise, the limitation period again applies regardless of age.[23] Similarly, California requires medical tort actions by minors to be commenced within three years from the date of the wrongful act but permits minors under six to commence

20. Miss. Code Ann. § 15-1-36(2).
21. Cal. Civ. Proc. Code § 340.5.
22. Ala. Code § 6-5-482(b).
23. Tex. Civ. Prac. & Rem. Code § 74.251(a).

actions within the greater period of three years from the wrongful act or the minor's eighth birthday.[24] Other jurisdictions, such as Arizona, Illinois, and the District of Columbia, take a more expansive approach by discounting any time in which the claimant was younger than age 18.[25] However, as further discussed below, statutes of repose may preclude a theoretical 18-plus-year reprieve.

As with minors, many states provide a tolling period for persons who sustain injury during a period of permanent or temporary disability.[26] Many provisions concerning disability, such as the District of Columbia's, neatly coexist with provisions pertaining to minors and have general applicability to a variety of claims.[27] Disability provisions usually toll the limitations period until the removal of a disability, if it is one of a temporary nature; however, the upper limit on tolling is often the statute of repose.[28]

In addition to minors and persons with disabilities, nearly half of all U.S. states also have special tolling provisions for the discovery of foreign objects mistakenly placed inside a patient during surgery.[29] Though the misplacement of a foreign object would seem to implicate the basic discovery rule, foreign object provisions often serve as an explicit exception to it, providing time in addition to the initial limitation period. For instance, California's foreign body provision delays the initial three-year limitation entirely if a nontherapeutic "foreign body" has been left inside a patient.[30] California's rule theoretically gives that patient an unlimited time to discover or to use reasonable diligence to discover the presence of the "foreign body."[31] Often, a foreign object provision is intertwined with the discovery rule. New York requires that an action be commenced within one year of the date of discovery of the object, or the date of discovery of facts that would reasonably lead to discovery of the object, whichever is earlier.[32]

In cases where claimants can show that fraud, intentional concealment, or misrepresentation of relevant facts caused a delay in the discovery of the injury, additional time may be provided, sometimes indefinitely. Thirteen U.S. jurisdictions have some version of provisions addressing these scenarios: California, Florida, Illinois, Michigan, Mississippi, North Dakota, Oregon, South Carolina,

---

24. Cal. Civ. Proc. Code § 340.5.

25. Ariz. Rev. Stat. Ann. § 12-502; D.C. Code § 12–302(a)(1); 735 Ill. Comp. Stat. Ann. 5/13-212(b).

26. *E.g.*, 735 Ill. Comp. Stat. Ann. 5/13-212(c); Nev. Rev. Stat. § 11.250; Va. Code Ann. § 8.01-243(C)(3).

27. D.C. Code § 12–302.

28. *See, e.g.*, 735 Ill. Comp. Stat. Ann. 5/13-212(c)–(d).

29. Heather Morton, *Medical Liability/Malpractice Statutes of Limitation*, Nat'l Conf. of State Legis. (Mar. 20, 2014), http://www.ncsl.org/research/financial-services-and-commerce/medical-liability-malpractice-statutes-of-limitation.aspx.

30. Ashworth v. Mem. Hosp., 206 Cal. App. 3d 1047, 1058 (Ct. App. 1988).

31. *Id.*

32. N.Y. C.P.L.R. § 214-a.

Tennessee, Utah, Vermont, Virginia, and Washington.[33] As with other tolling provisions, fraud provisions can vary significantly in duration. Florida's statute, for example, provides that a claim may be tolled for two additional years beyond the discovery of the injury where it can be shown that fraud, concealment, or intentional misrepresentation of fact prevented the discovery of the injury.[34] On the other hand, in Vermont, there is no upper limitation in cases of fraud or intentional concealment.[35]

Finally, procedural presuit tolling periods may operate to suspend the running of the statute of limitation, thereby creating a time period for potential litigants to evaluate claims and conduct presuit investigation and claim negotiation, as is the case in Florida,[36] Michigan,[37] and Tennessee.[38] The tolling period is commenced upon the service of a presuit notice of intent to initiate litigation to prospective defendants.[39] In Florida, for medical malpractice claims, service of a notice initiates a 90-day tolling period as to all potential defendants, during which time a complaint cannot be filed.[40] In that time, a presuit screening process takes place in which parties are permitted to conduct informal discovery, including unsworn statements, exchange of documents, written questions, and physical and mental examinations of claimants.[41] For claims against nursing homes and assisted living facilities, Florida provides a shorter presuit tolling period of 75 days.[42]

In Michigan, a 182-day presuit period is provided, during which time the statute of limitation is tolled only if it would have run during that period; otherwise, it is not tolled at all.[43] The 182-day tolling can be shortened to 91 days for a number of reasons, such as if the claimant has previously filed a complaint against any of the prospective defendants.[44] In Tennessee, a 120-day extension is provided to the statute of limitation *and* statute of repose upon the proper service of a notice of intent.[45] The takeaway from these provisions is that presuit notice and tolling peri-

---

33. Cal. Civ. Proc. Code § 340.5; 735 Ill. Comp. Stat. Ann. 5/13-212; Mich. Comp. Laws § 600.5838a(2)(a); Miss. Code Ann. § 15-1-36(2)(b); N.D. Cent. Code § 28-01-18(3); Or. Rev. Stat. § 12.110(4); S.C. Code Ann. § 15-3-545; Tenn. Code Ann. § 29-26-116(3); Utah Code Ann. § 78B-3-404(2)(b); Vt. Stat. Ann. tit. 12, § 521; Va. Code § 8.01-243; Wash. Rev. Code § 4.16.350(30).

34. Fla. Stat. Ann. § 95.11(b).

35. Vt. Stat. Ann. tit. 12, § 521.

36. *See* Fla. Stat. Ann. §§ 766.106, 400.0233, 429.293; Fla. R. Civ. P. 1.650.

37. *See* Mich. Comp. Laws §§ 600.2912b, 600.5856(c).

38. *See* Tenn. Code Ann. § 29-26-121.

39. Fla. Stat. Ann. § 766.106(4); Mich. Comp. Laws §§ 600.2912b, 600.5856(c).

40. Fla. Stat. Ann. § 766.106(4); Fla. R. Civ. P. 1.650.

41. Fla. Stat. Ann. § 766.106(6)(b)(1)–(6).

42. Fla. Stat. Ann. § 429.293(4). In all medical tort claims, at the end of presuit, the parties can extend the tolling by mutual agreement and, in doing so, the claimant may be entitled to an additional 60 days or the remainder of the period of the statute of limitation, whichever is greater, within which to file suit. Fla. Stat. Ann. §§ 766.106(4), 400.0233(4), 429.293(4); Fla. R. Civ. P. 1.650(d)(3).

43. Omelenchuk v. City of Warren, 609 N.W.2d 177, 181 (Mich. 2000).

44. Mich. Comp. Laws § 600.2912b(3)(a)–(d).

45. Tenn. Code Ann. § 29-26-121(c).

ods are not at all uniform and are calculated in complex ways from state to state. Careful reading and calculation of the periods are crucial.

In light of all the scenarios where a limitations period can be stretched, bent, and contorted through injury discovery and tolling rules, statutes of repose are meant to apply as an upper time limit and absolute bar to filing a medical tort claim (with some exceptions[46]). For states that do have a discrete repose period, repose provisions on medical tort claims are frequently shortened to curtail the volume of suits, but they vary considerably and can range up to a maximum of ten years, such as in Missouri, Nebraska, and Texas.[47]

As a result, a basic analysis of statutes of limitation and repose should first include determining all of the statutory or rule provisions that may apply to a medical tort claim. These can include different theories of recovery and may be separated further depending on the nature of services provided and the identities of prospective defendants. Next, a careful review of definitions is essential because special terms of art often apply to include or exclude certain claims in sometimes unpredictable ways. After that, analysis should turn to determining accrual of the cause of action based on either the basic date of injury or rules pertaining to discovery of the injury. Finally, consideration of any applicable tolling periods and the period of repose is essential. Because limitation and repose issues can be dispositive to a claim, counsel should always adopt a conservative approach to their calculations. For plaintiff counsel, such an approach should always rely on a determination of the earliest possible date. Defense counsel should be prepared to address all arguments that a later date applies.

When states permit an extension of the limitation or tolling period by mutual agreement, such agreements can be a beneficial lever when litigants believe resolution may be close at hand. Plaintiffs and defendants alike may wish to avoid the uncertainty and cost of a limitations battle when a claim appears to be otherwise meritorious.

In litigation, defense counsel's careful review of the complaint may reveal a limitations argument ripe for a motion to dismiss. This is especially true in instances where the discovery rule operates to shorten the default limitation period. A complaint may inadvertently plead a timeline of events indicating that an injury was apparent to the plaintiff while simultaneously contending that a later, more timely date applies. In discovery, defense counsel should draw out as much detail as possible to pinpoint the earliest date of accrual. Interrogatories and depositions should request the exact dates of evaluation, diagnosis, informed consent, and treatment; signs and symptoms of injury; and the exact time plaintiff became aware of any lapse in care or relevant injuries. Depositions are a crucial tool in issues of discovery and due diligence. A claimant's recall of when things first went wrong may differ from the facts pled in the complaint. Unequivocal testimony,

46. Most frequently, exceptions are made for minors. *E.g.*, Tenn. Code Ann. § 29-26-121(c). Fraud or intentional concealment can also circumvent the repose period. *E.g.*, Vt. Stat. Ann. tit. 12, § 521.

47. Mo. Rev. Stat. § 516.105; Neb. Rev. Stat. § 44-2828; Tex. Civ. Prac. & Rem. Code § 74.251(b).

such as "I knew something was wrong when . . . ," can provide key support to a motion for summary judgment or affirmative defenses on a limitation issue. Likewise, counsel for plaintiff should ask the identical questions during case intake and early assessment; verify answers gleaned with relevant medical records; and, after filing the complaint, review the established timeline of events in the complaint with the client as a part of preparation for deposition.

Medical Tort Damage Caps

Damage caps enacted as part of medical tort reform efforts have tended to focus on two types of damage awards: noneconomic damages and punitive damages. Both are addressed here.

Caps on noneconomic damages are perhaps the most familiar method of medical tort reform. These provide a maximum upper limit on recovery for damages, including pain and suffering, loss of society, emotional distress, loss of consortium, disfigurement, loss of childbearing capacity, loss of parental guidance, and loss of enjoyment of life.[48] Tort reform advocates cite the difficulty of juries in quantifying noneconomic damages and the mitigation of high malpractice insurance rates as policy reasons warranting caps.[49] Although the positive and negative effects of such caps are heavily debated, nearly two-thirds of all U.S. states have implemented some form of noneconomic damage caps in medical tort cases.[50] On the other hand, 16 jurisdictions—Alabama, Arizona, Arkansas, Connecticut, Delaware, the District of Columbia, Iowa, Kentucky, Minnesota, New Jersey, New York, Pennsylvania, Rhode Island, Vermont, Washington, and Wyoming—have no cap on noneconomic damages in medical tort claims.[51]

For states that have chosen to cap noneconomic damages, the most common cap level is a maximum recovery in the range of \$250,000 to \$500,000 per claimant or judgment, with the vast majority of jurisdictions adopting caps under \$1 million per claimant.[52] Many state statutes adopt a tiered cap approach based on a variety of factors, including whether injury includes severe or permanent physical impairment or death,[53] whether the defendant agrees to presuit arbitration of

48. Herbert M. Kritzer et al., *An Exploration of "Noneconomic" Damages in Civil Jury Awards*, 55 Wm. & Mary Law Rev. 974 (2014).

49. *Noneconomic Damages Reform*, Am. Tort Reform Ass'n, http://www.atra.org/issues/noneconomic-damages-reform (last visited Oct. 2, 2020).

50. Thomson Reuters, *50 State Statutory Surveys, Health Care: Medical Malpractice*, 0100 Surveys 45 (Sept. 2020).

51. *Id.*

52. *Id.*

53. Md. Code Ann., Cts. & Jud. Proc. § 3-2A-09; Mass. Gen. Laws ch. 231, § 60H; Mich. Comp. Laws Ann. § 600.1483; N.C. Gen. Stat. § 90-21.19(b)(1).

the claim,[54] and whether the defendant is an individual practitioner or an institutional provider.[55]

Furthermore, caps on noneconomic damages are subject to frequent political revisions and appellate litigation. Despite their state legislatures' efforts, the highest courts in Alabama, New Hampshire, and Washington have examined noneconomic damage caps, and each declared its respective state statutes unconstitutional.[56] Conversely, after a long period without caps on noneconomic damages, North Carolina enacted caps in medical malpractice cases on noneconomic damages in 2011.[57] As these examples make clear, practitioners should always monitor local policy debates and litigation, which change regularly with respect to noneconomic damages.

The vast majority of states permit some form of punitive damages in medical tort cases.[58] A small minority, including Nebraska,[59] Puerto Rico,[60] and Washington,[61] do not allow punitive damages for any civil claims accruing under the law of their jurisdictions. Further, two states specifically prohibit punitive damages in medical tort cases: Illinois does so in all medical tort cases,[62] while Oregon prohibits punitive damages against individual licensed health providers, but not against corporate entities, such as hospitals and nursing homes.[63]

From a practice standpoint, statutory language prohibiting punitive damages can be deceiving. For example, while Washington prohibits punitive damages for injury committed solely within the state, it allows the importation of the punitive damage laws of another state when the facts of a claim have a more significant relationship to the foreign state.[64] A Washington plaintiff might, for example, plead punitive damages in a nursing home malpractice claim based upon the acts or omissions of the corporate management, which might be a national company having facilities in a number of states. The plaintiff could then allege that relevant decisions were made by a management company in its home office outside of

54. FLA. STAT. ANN. §§ 766.207, 766.209(4)(a).

55. FLA. STAT. ANN. § 766.118(2)–(3); GA. CODE ANN. § 51-13-1(b)–(d); TEX. CIV. PRAC. & REM. CODE § 74.301.

56. Ray v. Anesthesia Assocs. of Mobile, 674 So. 2d 525 (Ala. 1995); Carson v. Maurer, 424 A.2d 825 (N.H. 1980); Sofie v. Fireboard Corp., 771 P.2d 711 (Wash. 1989).

57. The cap is $500,000 per plaintiff, regardless of number of defendants. N.C. GEN. STAT. § 90-21.19(a).

58. Paul Shearer, *Punitive Damage Awards, Caps, and Standards*, CONN. GEN. ASSEMBLY OFFICE OF LEGIS. RES. (Nov. 7, 2003), https://www.cga.ct.gov/2003/olrdata/ins/rpt/2003-R-0743.htm.

59. Miller v. Kingsley, 230 N.W.2d 472 (Neb. 1975).

60. NPR, Inc. v. Am. Int'l Ins. Co. of P.R., 242 F. Supp. 2d 121, 127 (D.P.R. 2003).

61. Dailey v. N. Coast Life Ins. Co., 919 P.2d 589, 590 (Wash. 1996); Barr v. Interbay Citizens Bank, 635 P.2d 441 (Wash. 1981).

62. 735 ILL. COMP. STAT. ANN. 5/2-1115.

63. OR. REV. STAT. § 31.740.

64. Kammerer v. W. Gear Corp., 635 P.2d 708, 711–12 (Wash. 1981); *Barr*, 635 P.2d at 443.

Washington. If that state (such as California or Florida) permitted punitive damages, the claimant could then conceivably seek such damages in Washington.[65]

Like other noneconomic damages, states that do permit claims for punitive damages in medical tort actions often adopt a tiered approach based upon the level of compensatory damages, the nature of the conduct involved, or the financial worth of the defendant.

While punitive damage claims can produce eye-popping awards, the U.S. Supreme Court reaffirmed the theoretical upper limit on punitive damages in the 2003 case of *State Farm Mutual Automobile Insurance Co. v. Campbell*.[66] In doing so, it overturned a $145 million Utah verdict against State Farm, holding that the judgment was excessive and violated the Due Process Clause of the 14th Amendment.[67] Relying on its prior decision in *BMW of North America, Inc. v. Gore*, the Court reasoned that any grant of punitive damages should be based on the following three factors: the degree of reprehensibility of the defendant's misconduct (noted as the most important factor), the disparity between the actual or potential harm suffered by the plaintiff and the punitive damages awarded, and the difference between the punitive damages awarded and the civil penalties authorized or imposed in comparable cases.[68] Examining these factors, it mused that a punitive damage award that is more than a single-digit multiplier of compensatory damages would likely implicate due process concerns, although the calculus would not function as a rigid benchmark.[69]

For practitioners in the vast majority of states that permit punitive damages, the mere prospect of such damages can dramatically affect the settlement value of a claim. Many states do not permit the pleading of punitive damages in the initial complaint, requiring that the plaintiff later move to plead for punitive damages and submit a proffer of evidence in support.[70] Some states permit a counterproffer by the defendant; others do not. Usually, only a reasonable basis is required to plead punitive damages. However, when punitive damages are permitted to be pled, such damages may dramatically raise the cost of litigation by subjecting defendants to intensive financial worth discovery.[71] Additionally, because of the potential for confusion of issues and prejudice concerning liability as opposed to issues of financial worth, defense counsel should consider a motion to bifurcate a trial into liability and damage phases.[72]

---

65. *Barr*, 635 P.2d at 443.
66. State Farm Mut. Auto. Ins. Co. v. Campbell, 538 U.S. 408 (2003).
67. *Id.* at 416–20.
68. *Id.* at 418–19 (citing BMW of N. Am., Inc. v. Gore, 517 U.S. 559, 575 (1996)).
69. *Id.* at 425.
70. *E.g.*, Fla. Stat. Ann. §§ 768.72, 400.0237; Minn. Stat. § 549.191.
71. *See* Globe Newspaper Co. v. King, 658 So. 2d 518 (Fla. 1995).
72. *See* Fed. R. Civ. P. 42(b); John T. Simpson, *Discovery of Net Worth in Bifurcated Punitive Damages Cases: A Suggested Approach after* Transportation Insurance Co. v. Moriel, 37 S. Tex. L. Rev. 193 (1996).

Certificates of Medical Merit

Certificate of merit statutes are thought to curtail frivolous medical tort claims by requiring either a professional legal or medical opinion supporting the claim, either concurrent with or subsequent to the filing of a complaint.[73] Just less than half of U.S. jurisdictions have no such requirement.[74] Among the majority of states that do require certificates of merit, the requirements vary significantly.[75] The approaches, however, fall into three general categories: those requiring certification of merit by an attorney upon filing the complaint, those requiring a certification or affidavit from a medical expert upon filing the complaint, and those requiring either of the prior two sometime after filing of the complaint.[76]

Typical of the first category, New York requires, upon filing of the complaint, the filing attorney to execute a certificate stating that the attorney has reviewed the facts of the case, has consulted with at least one healthcare provider licensed in New York who is knowledgeable of the subject matter and who has credentials similar to the defendant(s), and has concluded there is a reasonable basis for the claim.[77] The statute does provide exceptions for time constraints due to the statute of limitation or difficulties obtaining an expert.[78]

In the second category, a certificate of merit authored by a medical professional often requires information similar to expert testimony. This may include a recitation of the expert's qualifications and experience; the basis of opinion, including all relevant records reviewed; an opinion regarding the duty and standard of care incumbent upon all relevant defendant practitioners; an opinion identifying all breaches in the standard of care; a description of any resultant medical injury, past, present, and future; and a statement that all opinions are given within a reasonable degree of medical probability.[79]

Despite states' efforts to ensure the merit of any claim, bias concerns arise when the author of a certificate derives a substantial portion of her income from testifying in medical tort claims. Maryland, for example, has taken steps to address this concern by requiring experts who testify or author certificates of merit to include a certification that the expert devotes no more than 20 percent of her professional activities to those that involve testimony in personal injury claims.[80]

73. Benjamin Grossberg, *Uniformity, Federalism, and Tort Reform: The Erie Implication of Medical Malpractice Certificate of Merit Statutes*, 159 U. Pa. L. Rev. 217 (2010).

74. These are Alabama, Alaska, Arkansas, California, the District of Columbia, Idaho, Indiana, Iowa, Kansas, Kentucky, Louisiana, Maine, Massachusetts, Montana, Nebraska, New Hampshire, New Mexico, North Carolina, Oregon, Puerto Rico, Rhode Island, South Dakota, Washington, and Wisconsin. Heather Morton, *Medical Liability/Malpractice Statutes of Limitation*, Nat'l Conf. of State Legis. (Mar. 20, 2014), http://www.ncsl.org/research/financial-services-and-commerce/medical-liability-malpractice-statutes-of-limitation.aspx.

75. *Id.*

76. Grossberg, *supra* note 73, at 222–24.

77. N.Y. C.P.L.R. § 3012-a.

78. N.Y. C.P.L.R. § 3012-a(a)(2)–(3).

79. *See, e.g.*, Conn. Gen. Stat. Ann. § 52-190a; Md. Code Ann., Cts. & Jud. Proc. § 3-2A-04(b).

80. Md. Code Ann., Cts. & Jud. Proc. § 3-2A-04(b)(4).

Merit certification can present significant logistical challenges to claimants, and courts have recognized this fact. In 2009, the Washington Supreme Court invalidated that state's certificate of merit statute in a unanimous 9–0 decision, reasoning that the statute violated plaintiffs' constitutional right of access to the courts.[81] In doing so, it reasoned, in part, that such statutes essentially require plaintiffs to engage in discovery prior to filing a claim.[82]

Even before early case assessment, plaintiff and defense counsel should locate and thoroughly interview qualified experts in the areas in which they may receive cases. States' respective laws for qualification of experts and rules of evidence serve as key starting points for vetting experts. Depending on the jurisdiction, experts should be prepared to explain issues including the proportion of income derived from work as an expert; prior expert testimony in deposition, trial, and arbitration; prior personal litigation history and testimony involving relevant issues; whether the expert has been disqualified for any reason; the expert's rate of pay for various case tasks; and the approach usually taken in review of records and formulation of opinions.

Venue

With the panoply of state laws regarding when claims can be brought, the level of potential damages awarded, and the procedural hurdles for filing, it stands to reason that some venues are more attractive than others. Advocates of narrowed venue rules seek to curtail "venue shopping," wherein a plaintiff may seek out a potentially more hospitable venue, despite a less than solid connection to the facts of the case. Advocates of broad venue rules cite the importance of the right to choose the appropriate forum for redress of injury. Naturally, there are as many iterations to the law of venue as there are reasons for selection.

While medical tort claims tend to have a more local focus, various venue issues can arise in multiparty litigation where there are a number of defendants or where one or more defendants is a corporation. Recognizing this, a handful of states have taken measures to restrict venue in medical malpractice cases. Arkansas, for example, has enacted venue provisions requiring that any civil action for medical injury against a medical provider be filed in the county in which the alleged act or omission occurred.[83] Similar to Arkansas, Pennsylvania and Mississippi have also adopted restrictions on venue in medical malpractice cases, providing that a medical professional liability or negligence action may be brought against a healthcare provider only in a county in which the cause of action arose.[84] The large majority of jurisdictions, including California, Florida, and Texas, have no specific venue restrictions on medical tort claims.

81. Putnam v. Wenatchee Med. Ctr., 216 P.3d 374 (Wash. 2009).
82. *Id.* at 376–80.
83. ARK. CODE ANN. § 16-55-213(e).
84. PA. R. CIV. P. No. 1006(a)(1); MISS. CODE ANN. § 11-11-3(3).

Efforts to restrict venue have not been limited to state legislatures. Institutional and individual providers have in many instances taken venue into their own hands. In attempts to mitigate the risk of not just unfavorable locales, but of jury trials themselves, a growing proportion of medical providers have elected to use arbitration agreements and forum selection clauses in admitting agreements.[85]

One of the most important considerations in choice of venue is the availability of witnesses. When care is provided in an institutional setting, the claimant may have interacted with several, even dozens of, caregivers during the course of treatment. Turnover in some care settings can be significant.[86] Depending on the age of the claim, key caregivers may have changed jobs and relocated outside the jurisdiction.

Additionally, the capacity of the court to handle claims is an important factor. Medical tort claims routinely require extensive discovery, including the testimony of numerous fact and expert witnesses. They also often include vigorous motion practice, complex fact presentations, and lengthy instructions for juries. In some jurisdictions, dockets move slowly because of lack of resources or overall caseload. Many local court jurisdictions in larger metropolitan areas have specialized sections for complex claims. Technological capacity and understanding can vary significantly among neighboring venues. When a choice of venue exists, the ability of the courts to manage the intricate nature of medical tort claims from a substantive, procedural, and technical standpoint is essential to maximizing the results for clients.

Conclusion

The effects of several decades of nationwide tort reform have shaped a legal landscape that is varied and ever shifting, but not impassible. For statutes of limitation, the terms of art employed are unique to medical torts and reflect states' various efforts to include and exclude certain parties and claims. Reform efforts have placed constraints on noneconomic and punitive damages in many jurisdictions, but others have little to no upper limit. Certificates of merit require a close and early examination of medical records and early conference with experts to thoroughly understand medical issues, which are critical to many components of a successful claim or defense. When faced with a choice of venue, like any claim, the availability of essential documents, testimony, and court capacity are central to obtaining the best possible result for clients.

85. Elizabeth Rolph et al., *Arbitration Agreements in Health Care: Myths and Reality*, 60 Law & Contemp. Probs. 153, 160 (1997).

86. *See* Olalya Ayanna Bryant, Employee Turnover in the Long-Term Care Industry (Feb. 2017) (Ph.D. dissertation, Walden University), https://scholarworks.waldenu.edu/cgi/viewcontent.cgi?article=4492&context=dissertations.

6

PRIVILEGE

Jacqueline Promislo

Just as in other industries, healthcare providers have an interest in keeping certain information confidential and protected from disclosure. This chapter explores four different privileges: the investigative privilege, the common interest privilege and the related joint defense privilege, peer review privileges, and the quality assurance privilege. Whether in the context of anticipated or existing litigation, an internal or government investigation, or obligations under federal law, it is important to understand the scope of these privileges, including potential pitfalls, so that lawyers are better able to advise their clients.

The first three privileges examined in this chapter are rooted in the attorney-client privilege. The primary purpose of the attorney-client privilege is to encourage "full and frank communication between attorneys and their clients."[1] The elements of the attorney-client privilege are that the person asserting the privilege is or seeks to become a client, the person to whom communication was made is an attorney or the attorney's subordinate, the communication relates to a fact of which the attorney was informed by the client in confidence, the communication is for the purpose of seeking legal advice, and the privilege has not been waived.[2] The burden is on the proponent to demonstrate that the attorney-client privilege applies.[3] If it applies, then communications between attorney and client will receive absolute and complete protection from disclosure, unless or until the privilege is waived.[4] Because the attorney-client privilege can obstruct the truth-finding process, it is narrowly construed.[5]

Investigative Privilege

Protecting the attorney-client privilege in the context of internal investigations is increasingly important as the healthcare industry wrestles with an ever-expanding regulatory landscape. Because of this increased regulation, healthcare providers are often compelled to investigate various compliance and regulatory issues.

1. Westinghouse Elec. Corp. v. Republic of Phil., 951 F.2d 1414, 1423 (3d Cir. 1991).
2. United States v. United Shoe Mach. Corp., 89 F. Supp. 357 (D. Mass. 1950).
3. United States v. Stern, 511 F.2d 1364, 1367 (2d Cir. 1975), *cert. denied*, 423 U.S. 829 (1975).
4. *In re* Grand Jury Proceedings, 102 F.3d 748, 750 (4th Cir. 1996).
5. *Westinghouse*, 951 F.2d at 1423.

Frequently, the impetus for the investigation is a subpoena or other governmental inquiry. Accordingly, attorneys must stay abreast of the potential limits on the attorney-client privilege in the context of internal investigations to provide sound legal advice on best practices for conducting an internal investigation.

The Supreme Court's decision in *Upjohn Co. v. United States* is the starting point for an examination of the parameters of the attorney-client privilege in the context of internal investigations. In *Upjohn*, independent auditors informed the company's in-house counsel that improper payments had been made to foreign government officials.[6] As a result, in-house counsel, together with outside counsel, conducted an internal investigation of the alleged wrongdoing. As part of the investigation, Upjohn attorneys sent questionnaires to all of its foreign managers, including lower-level managers. The IRS then sought all of the files relating to the investigation.[7] The Supreme Court held that the company's internal investigation was privileged and gave broad protection to the confidential communication of any corporate employee with its attorneys.[8] This broad shield included not only the "control group," such as high-level managers, but also lower-level managers. In rejecting the control group test, the court noted that lower-level employees are often the ones who possess the information needed by the corporation's lawyers.[9]

Chief Justice Burger's concurrence in *Upjohn* explained that former employees could also fall under the protection when the former employee speaks, at management's direction, with an attorney regarding conduct or proposed conduct within the scope of employment.[10] While some lower courts have followed this view,[11] others have not.[12] Overall, courts define "the corporate client" very broadly. Moreover, it is well settled that courts will protect communications to investigators, accountants, and others as long as they are operating under the direct supervision of an attorney.[13]

---

6. Upjohn Co. v. United States, 449 U.S. 383 (1981).
7. *Id.* at 388.
8. *Id.* at 384.
9. *Id.* at 391.
10. *Id.* at 403 (Burger, J., concurring).
11. *See* Admiral Ins. Co. v. U.S. Dist. Ct., 881 F.2d 1486, 1493 (9th Cir. 1989); *In re* Coordinated Pretrial Proceedings in Petroleum Prod. Antitrust Litig., 658 F.2d 1355, 1361 n.7 (9th Cir. 1981), *cert. denied*, 455 U.S. 990 (1982) (The *Upjohn* "rationale applies to the ex-employees . . . involved in this case. Former employees, as well as current employees, may possess the relevant information needed by corporate counsel to advise the client."); Amarin Plastics, Inc. v. Maryland Cup Corp., 116 F.R.D. 36, 41 (D. Mass. 1987) ("In some circumstances, the communications between a former employee and a corporate party's counsel may be privileged."); Porter v. Arco Metals Co., 642 F. Supp. 1116, 1118 (D. Mont. 1986) (*Upjohn* indicates that "the attorney-client privilege may extend to [defendant's] former employees . . . [with regard to their communications with] the company's counsel."); United States v. King, 536 F. Supp. 253, 259 (C.D. Cal. 1982) ("[An attorney-client] relationship existed even though [the witness] was not an employee of [the client] at the time of the conversation."), *overruled on other grounds*, United States v. Zolin, 842 F.2d 1135 (9th Cir. 1988).
12. *See, e.g.*, Barrett Indus. Trucks, Inc. v. Old Republic Ins. Co., 129 F.R.D. 515, 517–18 (N.D. Ill. 1990); Connolly Data Sys., Inc. v. Victor Techs., Inc., 114 F.R.D. 89, 93–94 (S.D. Cal. 1987).
13. *See* United States v. McPartlin, 595 F.2d 1321, 1336 (7th Cir. 1979).

Additionally, communications are protected only where a client or potential client requests, and the attorney gives, legal advice. However, investigations can constitute legal work.[14] In *In re Allen*, the Fourth Circuit noted that clients often retain lawyers to perform investigative work because they want the benefit of a lawyer's expertise and judgment, and if a client retains an attorney for their legal expertise to conduct an investigation, that lawyer is performing legal work.[15]

Most courts stress, however, that the privilege is not applicable in situations where the attorney merely gives business advice to her client.[16] The D.C. Circuit most recently examined this potential limitation on the privilege in the context of internal investigations.[17] In *In re Kellogg Brown & Root, Inc.*, the court reversed the district court after holding that documents created pursuant to an internal investigation were not privileged because they were not created for the primary purpose of giving legal advice. The district court first held that the documents failed a so-called "but-for" test, meaning that the documents were not solely created for the purpose of giving legal advice because KBR conducted the internal investigation in order to comply with Department of Defense regulations.[18] The appellate court rejected this test, concluding that such a test "would eradicate the attorney-client privilege for internal investigations conducted by businesses that are required by law to maintain compliance programs."[19] *KBR* established that if a corporation undertakes an internal investigation that is mandated by federal regulations, the investigation can be privileged, as long as one of the significant purposes of the internal investigation was obtaining or providing legal advice.[20]

In holding that the privilege did apply, the D.C. Circuit, in *KBR*, rejected several other distinctions that the district court had drawn between *Upjohn* and *KBR*, finding the two cases materially indistinguishable.[21] The district court attempted to tease out the following differences: the KBR investigation was done solely at the instructions of in-house counsel, nonattorneys helped conduct the investigation, and employees were not expressly informed that the purpose of the interviews was to assist the company in obtaining legal advice.[22] The D.C. Circuit held that the absence of outside counsel did not dilute the privilege.[23] However, commentators

14. *In re* Allen, 106 F.3d 582, 602 (4th Cir. 1997).

15. *Id.* at 604.

16. *In re* John Doe Corp., 675 F.2d 482, 488 (2nd Cir. 1982); *see In re* Grand Jury Subpoena Duces Tecum, 731 F.2d 1032, 1036–37 (2d Cir. 1984).

17. *In re* Kellogg Brown & Root, Inc., 756 F.3d 754 (D.C. Cir. 2014), *cert. denied sub nom.* United States *ex rel.* Barko v. Kellogg Brown & Root, Inc., 135 S. Ct. 1163 (2015).

18. *Id.* at 757.

19. *Id.* at 759.

20. *Id.* at 760.

21. *Id.* at 757.

22. *Id.* at 758.

23. The *KBR* decision on this point appears to have implicitly overruled an earlier case decided in the D.C. Circuit—*United States v. ISS Marine Servs., Inc.*, 905 F. Supp. 2d 121 (D.D.C. 2012). In *ISS Marine*, the court declined to extend the attorney-client privilege to an internal audit report created for a U.S. defense contractor. *Id.* at 124. Crucial to the court's analysis, the audit was done without input of

note that retaining outside counsel for internal investigations is a good practice to strengthen the privilege.[24] Further, the Court of Appeals noted that nonattorneys are routinely protected if they operate at the direction of counsel. Finally, the court noted that nothing in *Upjohn* required specific "magic words" to employees in order for the privilege to attach.[25]

Waiver of the Investigative Privilege

Generally, courts agree that information disclosed to a third party waives the investigative privilege. However, courts are split on how to handle waiver where the party claiming the privilege previously disclosed information discovered in an internal investigation to the government and a third party later wants to discover the information on the basis that any privilege was waived. In *KBR*, the relator in a qui tam action sought production of documents through an alleged waiver of the attorney-client privilege under Federal Rule of Evidence 412. Rule 412 provides that where a witness has used a writing to refresh memory before testifying, the adverse party is entitled to have the writing produced, as well as to introduce into evidence any portion of the writing that relates to the witness's testimony, if the court decides that justice requires the party to have them.[26] In *KBR*, the relator took the deposition of a corporate representative on the topic of the internal investigation. During the deposition, the witness testified that he reviewed documents relating to the internal investigation in preparation for his deposition. The relator took the position that because the witness reviewed the documents, as opposed to being provided with a summary of the documents, he waived the privilege. The

---

outside counsel. *Id.* at 130. The court stressed that outside counsel was not engaged in conducting the investigation, though there was an engagement letter indicating that outside counsel would "support the investigation for purposes of advising" the company of its legal obligations. *Id.* Applying a but-for test, the court concluded that the audit report was created for a business purpose—investigating concerns raised by employees—not to obtain legal advice. *KBR* unquestionably held: "The but-for test . . . is not appropriate for attorney-client privilege analysis." *In re* Kellogg Brown & Root, Inc., 756 F.3d at 759. Critical to the *ISS Marine* court's determination was the company's decision not to include counsel in conducting the investigation, while retaining counsel for the investigation in order to artificially "cloak the investigation with privilege." *ISS Marine Servs., Inc.*, 905 F. Supp. 2d at 129. The court further noted that the interviewed employees were not told that their responses would be transmitted to counsel for the purpose of securing legal advice and that the defendants made no showing that legal advice resulted from sending the audit report to outside counsel. *Id.*

In attempting to reconcile "other cases, [where the Circuit] appears to adopt a more 'lenient' standard," the D.C. Circuit further explained the holding of *ISS Marine* in its decision in *Wadelton v. Dep't of State*, 106 F. Supp. 3d 139 (D.D.C. 2015). Specifically, the court explained that the privilege did not extend in *ISS Marine* because, in addition to counsel not being involved in the report, "the government was years away from conducting its own investigation, and there was no indication that the employees who initially reported the possible fraud had any intention of bringing whistleblower claims." *Id.* at 152.

24. 2 McLaughlin on Class Actions § 11:3 (11th ed.).
25. *In re* Kellogg Brown & Root, Inc., 756 F.3d at 758.
26. *In re* Kellogg Brown & Root, Inc., 796 F.3d 137, 143 (D.C. Cir. 2015).

Court of Appeals described this argument as "absurd" and held that such logic would permit attorney-client privilege and work-product protection covering internal investigations to be defeated routinely by a counterparty noticing a deposition on the topic of the privileged nature of the internal investigation.[27]

The relator in *KBR* also argued that the attorney-client privilege was waived when KBR referenced the internal investigation in its motion for summary judgment such that it put the documents "at issue." Such waivers are certainly possible.[28] However, the court in *KBR* held that the mere mention of the internal investigation did not place the documents "at issue."[29]

The more critical concern over waiver of privilege relative to internal investigations is where a report detailing the findings of an internal investigation is disclosed to the government and a third party then seeks discovery of the report, claiming that privilege was waived when the report was provided to the government. Of course, generally, privileged information revealed to a third party does waive the privilege. However, the Eighth Circuit created an exception to this rule that has been analyzed, discussed, debated, and distinguished ever since.[30] The Sixth Circuit has even gone so far as to state that the case law in this area is in a state of "hopeless confusion."[31]

In *Diversified Industries, Inc. v. Meredith*, the Eighth Circuit held that after a party to the current lawsuit previously disclosed documents from an internal investigation to the SEC, the resulting waiver was limited because the privilege was waived only as to the government but was not waived as to other third parties. The Eighth Circuit stated, "To hold otherwise may have the effect of thwarting the developing procedure of corporations to employ independent outside counsel to investigate and advise them in order to protect stockholders, potential stockholders and customers."[32] Generally speaking, the First, Second (mostly), Third, Fourth, Sixth, Seventh (mostly), Tenth, and D.C. Circuits have rejected the idea of "limited waiver."[33] The Ninth Circuit has left the question open, though

---

27. *Id.* at 144.

28. *See* Koumoulis v. Indep. Fin. Mktg. Grp., Inc., 295 F.R.D. 28, 40 (E.D.N.Y. 2013), *aff'd*, 29 F. Supp. 3d 142 (E.D.N.Y. 2014) ("Both the attorney-client and work-product privileges may be waived if a party puts the privileged communication at issue by relying on it to support a claim or defense.").

29. *In re* Kellogg Brown & Root, Inc., 796 F.3d at 144.

30. *See* Diversified Indus., Inc. v. Meredith, 572 F.2d 596, 611 (8th Cir. 1977).

31. *In re* Columbia/HCA Healthcare Corp. Billing Practices Litig., 293 F.3d 289, 295 (6th Cir. 2002).

32. *Diversified Indus., Inc.*, 572 F.2d at 611.

33. United States v. Mass. Inst. of Tech., 129 F.3d 681 (1st Cir. 1997) (holding that the university's prior disclosure of its billing and other records to the auditing wing of the U.S. Department of Defense waived the privilege as to those documents in a subsequent request by the IRS); *see In re* Steinhardt Partners, L.P., 9 F.3d 230 (2d Cir. 1993) (finding that plaintiffs in a civil suit were entitled to a legal memorandum submitted to the SEC by Steinhardt in an attempt to forestall enforcement proceedings; because Steinhardt had voluntarily disclosed the memo to the SEC, the privilege was waived as to third party, but the Second Circuit did not adopt a per se rule against selective waiver); Westinghouse Elec. Corp. v. Republic of the Phil., 951 F.2d 1414 (3d Cir. 1991) (finding that voluntary disclosure of an

it has rejected it in specific cases.[34] To date, the Fifth and Eleventh Circuits have remained silent on this issue.

Judge Posner summarized why he believes courts have rejected selective waiver in *Dellwood Farms, Inc. v. Cargill, Inc.*, stating that there is a "fear that selective disclosure will be used to obtain a strategic advantage, and puzzlement why if the information is really confidential it was disclosed except for some nefarious strategic purpose."[35] The courts in the Seventh Circuit, however, disagree in their approach since the appellate court has been hesitant to create a per se rule against selective waiver.[36] In *Lawrence E. Jaffe Pension Plan v. Household International, Inc.*, the court found that selective waiver may be appropriate where the disclosing party took steps to preserve its privilege prior to voluntarily disclosing it to the SEC. Prior to disclosure, a bank and the SEC entered into a confidentiality agreement that expressly stated that "neither the Committee nor Household intend to waive the protections of the attorney work product doctrine, attorney-client privilege, or any other privilege applicable as to third parties."[37] Based on the confidentiality agreement, the court in *Jaffe* concluded that the bank took appropriate steps to preserve the confidentiality of attorney documents and denied a motion to compel.

On the other hand, courts in the Seventh Circuit have rejected selective waiver when it appeared a defendant made the disclosure to obtain a strategic advantage.[38] The court ultimately held that the policy reasons for disallowing selective waiver in that case outweighed the reasons for allowing it.

The Third Circuit rejected the idea of selective waiver, stating that "[i]f clients themselves divulge such information to third parties, chances are that they would

---

internal investigation report to the SEC and the Department of Justice during a bribery investigation waived privilege as to third party); *In re* Martin Marietta Corp., 856 F.2d 619 (4th Cir. 1988) (disclosure of an internal report to the U.S. attorney responding to allegations of fraud waived privilege and thus was discoverable by an indicted employee for use as a defense against charges arising out of same allegations); *In re* Fluor Intercontinental, Inc., 2020 U.S. App. LEXIS 9621, at *13 (4th Cir. 2020) (disclosure of internal report to government did not constitute waiver where there was no evidence to suggest that statements in the disclosure "quoted privileged communications or summarized them in substance and format"); *In re* Columbia/HCA Healthcare Corp., 293 F.3d 289, 302 (6th Cir. 2002) (rejecting the concept of selective waiver in any of its various forms); Burden-Meeks v. Welch, 319 F.3d 897, 899 (7th Cir. 2003) (holding selective disclosure is not an option but did not overrule *Dellwood Farms, Inc. v. Cargill, Inc.*, 128 F.3d 1122, 1126–27 (7th Cir. 1997)); *In re* Qwest Commc'ns Int'l Inc., 450 F.3d 1179, 1192 (10th Cir. 2006) (rejecting selective waiver in this specific case); Permian Corp. v. United States, 665 F.2d 1214, 1221 (D.C. Cir. 1981) (rejecting the argument that some public policy imperative inherent in the SEC's regulatory program requires that the traditional waiver doctrine be overridden).

34. United States v. Bergonzi, 403 F.3d 1048, 1050 (9th Cir. 2005).

35. *Dellwood Farms*, 128 F.3d at 1127.

36. *See, e.g.*, Lawrence E. Jaffe Pension Plan v. Household Int'l, Inc., 244 F.R.D. 412, 432 (N.D. Ill. 2006).

37. *Id.*

38. United States *ex rel.* Garbe v. Kmart Corp., No. 312CV00881MJRPMF, 2014 WL 2218758, at *3–4 (S.D. Ill. May 29, 2014) ("K–Mart concluded that the potential benefits outweighed the risk. It now seeks [to] withhold the same information it produced to an adversary from another adversary.").

also have divulged it to their attorneys, even without the protection of the privilege. Thus, once a client has revealed privileged information to a third party, the basic justification for the privilege no longer applies . . . ."[39]

Likewise, in rejecting selective waiver, the D.C. Circuit observed that it could not see how the availability of a selective waiver would serve the interests underlying the attorney-client privilege.[40] The court reasoned that selective waiver "has little to do with" the privilege's purpose—protecting the confidentiality of attorney-client communications in order to encourage clients to obtain informed legal assistance. The court explained that while voluntary cooperation with government investigations "may be a laudable activity, . . . it is hard to understand how such conduct improves the attorney-client relationship."[41]

A district court in Arizona examined the issue of selective waiver in a healthcare-related case.[42] In *Bickler v. Senior Lifestyle Corp.*, the United States District Court for the District of Arizona held that information pertaining to an internal investigation in a nursing home, which was later revealed to the Department of Health Services (DHS), remained privileged information despite the disclosure.[43] Two nursing home patients were injured, and the nursing home conducted an investigation, which was undertaken at the direction of in-house counsel and performed by the HR department. The investigation consisted of contacting 18 employees, who responded to questions posed during interviews, and their answers were summarized on a form that included the questions, which resulted in a timeline of relevant events including a short summary of the interviews. The HR manager then prepared a report that was forwarded with the other materials to in-house counsel.

The results of the investigation were later turned over to the DHS. Plaintiffs contended that the communication lost its privilege when the defendant shared the investigative materials with the DHS. The court disagreed and noted that the Arizona Court of Appeals had declined to follow the blanket rule that a privilege is waived when privileged materials are shared with the government.[44] *Danielson v. Superior Court* held that the physician-patient privilege was not lost when medical information was shared with the Arizona Board of Medical Examiners. The court of appeals explained that Arizona policy, as reflected in Arizona statutes, clearly favored full communication with this governmental entity. The court also closely compared the physician-patient privilege with the attorney-client privilege, ultimately holding that the privilege was not waived.[45]

39. Westinghouse Elec. Corp. v. Republic of the Phil., 951 F.2d 1414, 1424 (3d Cir. 1991).
40. Permian Corp. v. United States, 665 F.2d 1214, 1220 (D.C. Cir. 1981).
41. *Id.*
42. Bickler v. Senior Lifestyle Corp., 266 F.R.D. 379, 381 (D. Ariz. 2010).
43. *Id.* at 384.
44. *Id.* at 382 (citing Danielson v. Super. Ct., 754 P.2d 1145 (Ariz. 1987)).
45. *Danielson*, 754 P.2d at 1149.

Protection of Attorney Work Product in the Context of Internal Investigations

The work-product privilege protects documents created by an attorney or at the attorney's direction in anticipation of litigation.[46] The attorney work-product privilege "shelters the mental processes of the attorney, providing a privileged area within which he can analyze and prepare his client's case."[47] Unlike the attorney-client privilege, protection of attorney work product is not limited to communications.[48] Also protected from disclosure are an attorney's thought processes and mental impressions, but there are limits on the extent to which attorneys may piggyback on the fact-finding investigations of their potentially more diligent (non-lawyer) counterparts.[49] And because it looks to the vitality of the adversary system rather than simply seeking to preserve confidentiality, the work-product privilege is not automatically waived by disclosure to a third party.[50]

Courts have focused quite a bit on what constitutes work performed "in anticipation of litigation." Generally, courts hold that an attorney's work is "in anticipation of litigation" as long as the attorney has "an eye toward litigation."[51] A district court in New York, considering this issue in the context of an internal investigation, reasoned that if, in light of the nature of the document and the factual situation in the particular case, the document can fairly be said to have been prepared or obtained because of the prospect of litigation, the privilege attaches.[52] The court noted that a work product that "might also help in preparation for litigation" will not be protected by the work-product doctrine if it was "prepared in the ordinary course of business" or "would have been created in essentially similar form irrespective of the litigation."[53]

The D.C. Circuit recognizes the because-of test, in this regard, holding that material generated in anticipation of litigation may also be used for ordinary business purposes without losing its protected status.[54] This aspect of the work-product doctrine allows courts to extend work-product protection to a document that "serves multiple purposes, so long as the protected material was prepared because of the prospect of litigation."[55]

---

46. Koumoulis v. Indep. Fin. Mktg. Grp., Inc., 295 F.R.D. 28, 39 (E.D.N.Y. 2013), *aff'd*, 29 F. Supp. 3d 142 (E.D.N.Y. 2014) (citing *In re* Grand Jury Subpoenas Dated March 19, 2002 & August 2, 2002, 318 F.3d 379, 383 (2d Cir. 2003)).
47. United States v. Nobles, 422 U.S. 225 (1975).
48. *In re* Sealed Case, 676 F.2d 793, 809 (D.C. Cir. 1982).
49. Sandra T.E. v. S. Berwyn Sch. Dist. 100, 600 F.3d 612, 622 (7th Cir. 2010).
50. *Id.*
51. *Id.* at 622.
52. Koumoulis v. Indep. Fin. Mktg. Grp., Inc., 295 F.R.D. 28, 39 (E.D.N.Y. 2013).
53. *Id.*
54. United States v. ISS Marine Servs., Inc., 905 F. Supp. 2d 121, 134 (D.D.C. 2012) (finding that an internal audit had an obvious business purpose and that minimal involvement of counsel questioned whether document would meet the standard).
55. *Id.*

Further, there is no requirement that a specific claim be filed or even considered, as that would undermine a lawyer's effectiveness at a particularly critical stage of the legal representation. It goes without saying that if a party threatens suit, an internal investigation would clearly be in anticipation of litigation.[56]

However, in limited situations, documents protected as attorney work product are nonetheless discoverable if a party can establish a "substantial need" for the documents and cannot obtain equivalent materials without "undue hardship."[57] Specifically, Federal Rule 26(b) states:

> Protection Against Disclosure. If the court orders discovery of those materials, it must protect against disclosure of the mental impressions, conclusions, opinions, or legal theories of a party's attorney or other representative concerning the litigation.[58]

Essentially, Rule 26 breaks work product into two categories—fact and opinion. Fact work product can be discovered with the showing of substantial need, as explained above. However, opinion work product (mental impressions, conclusions, and theories) is given greater protection by the courts. Disclosure of witness interviews and related documents is particularly discouraged.[59] While actual disclosure of pure mental impressions may be deemed waiver, and while there may be indirect waiver in extreme circumstances, generally such work product is not subject to discovery.[60]

Waiver of Work-Product Protection

Similar to attorney-client privilege, a party may also waive work-product protection.[61] It appears, however, that only the Fourth Circuit has applied selective waiver in the context of *opinion* work product.[62] In *In re Martin Marietta Corp.*, the court concluded that the company made testimonial use of nonopinion work product by disclosing it to the government and that the waiver was comprehensive. Noting

---

56. *See* United States v. Reyes, 239 F.R.D. 591, 596 (N.D. Cal. 2006); *see also* Theodore R. Lotchin, *No Good Deed Goes Unpunished? Establishing a Self-Evaluative Privilege for Corporate Internal Investigations*, 46 Wm. & Mary L. Rev. 1137, 1155 (2004) ("Although the privilege is firmly established, courts are cognizant of the special considerations that an internal corporate investigation presents. In fact, '[m]ost courts have recognized that once the suspicion of wrongdoing rises to the level where an internal investigation is commissioned, litigation is virtually inevitable . . . .'").

57. Fed. R. Civ. P. 26.

58. Fed. R. Civ. P. 26.

59. Sandra T.E. v. S. Berwyn Sch. Dist. 100, 600 F.3d 612, 622–23 (7th Cir. 2010) (citing Upjohn Co. v. United States, 449 U.S. 383, 398–99 (1981)) ("Forcing an attorney to disclose notes and memoranda of witnesses' oral statements is particularly disfavored because it tends to reveal the attorney's mental processes . . . .").

60. *In re* Martin Marietta Corp., 856 F.2d 619, 626 (4th Cir. 1988).

61. United States v. Reyes, 239 F.R.D. 591, 603 (N.D. Cal. 2006) ("Likewise, the Court finds [the parties] gave up their work-product privilege when they shared the substance of their work product with the government.").

62. *In re Martin Marietta Corp.*, 856 F.2d 619.

that opinion work product generally receives greater protection from the courts, however, and that Federal Rule of Civil Procedure 26(b)(3) suggests special protection for opinion work product, the court declined to hold that the company had waived work-product protection for opinion work product.[63]

Notably, the circuit that created selective waiver for attorney-client privilege rejected the theory in the context of nonopinion (fact) work product. In *In re Chrysler Motors Corp. Overnight Evaluation Program Litigation*, the company produced a computer tape to its adversaries in civil litigation under a nonwaiver/confidentiality agreement.[64] When the government sought production of the computer tape from the plaintiffs, the company protested. The Eighth Circuit determined that the tape was not opinion work product. It then held that "Chrysler waived any work product protection by voluntarily disclosing the computer tape to its adversaries, the class action plaintiffs, during the due diligence phase of the settlement negotiations."[65]

The First Circuit also rejected selective waiver for nonopinion work product, stating that "it would take better reason than we have to depart from the prevailing rule that disclosure to an adversary, real or potential, forfeits work product protection."[66] The Third Circuit held that a selective waiver is foreign to the objectives underlying the work-product doctrine, noting that attorneys are free to prepare their cases without fear of disclosure to an adversary, as long as they and their clients refrain from making such disclosures themselves.[67] Finally, the Sixth Circuit concluded that "[m]any of the reasons for disallowing selective waiver in the attorney-client privilege context also apply to the work product doctrine. The ability to prepare one's case in confidence . . . has little to do with talking to the Government."[68] The D.C. Circuit, Tenth Circuit, and Second Circuit have left the question open.[69]

Joint Defense or Common Interest Privilege

The joint defense or community-of-interest privilege[70] allows attorneys representing different clients with similar legal interests to share information without

63. *Id.* at 626.

64. *In re* Chrysler Motors Corp. Overnight Evaluation Program Litig., 860 F.2d 844, 845 (8th Cir. 1988).

65. *Id.* at 846.

66. United States v. Mass. Inst. of Tech., 129 F.3d 681, 687 (1st Cir. 1997).

67. Westinghouse Elec. Corp. v. Republic of the Phil., 951 F.2d 1414, 1429 (3d Cir. 1991).

68. *In re* Columbia/HCA Healthcare Corp. Billing Practices Litig., 293 F.3d 289, 306 (6th Cir. 2002).

69. *See In re* Subpoenas Duces Tecum, 738 F.2d 1367, 1371 (D.C. Cir. 1984); *In re* Qwest Commc'ns Int'l Inc., 450 F.3d 1179, 1190–91 (10th Cir. 2006); *In re* Steinhardt Partners, L.P., 9 F.3d 230, 235 (2d Cir. 1993); *but see* FED. R. EVID. § 502(b) (disclosure does not operate as waiver when inadvertent, the holder of the privilege took reasonable steps to prevent the disclosure, and the holder promptly took reasonable steps to rectify the error).

70. Several circuits suggest that the joint defense privilege should really be referred to as the "common interest" or the "community-of-interest" privilege. *See In re* Grand Jury Subpoena, 274 F.3d 563,

being required to disclose it to others, allowing the information shared between the cooperating attorneys to be privileged and nondiscoverable.[71] Joint defense can be seen as an extension of the attorney-client privilege.[72] In essence, the joint defense privilege provides an exception to the general rule that disclosure of privileged information to a third party acts as a waiver of the privilege. Further, a joint defense privilege cannot be waived without the consent of all parties who share the privilege.[73] However, a party to joint defense communications may waive the attorney-client privilege by disclosing such confidential information to persons outside the scope of the joint defense relationship.[74]

The common interest privilege applies in civil and criminal litigation, as well as in purely transactional contexts.[75] The burden rests on the party asserting the privilege to establish its existence by showing that the communications were made in the course of a joint defense effort, the statements were designed to further the effort, and the privilege has not been waived.[76] Moreover, and more importantly, to qualify for and to maintain the privilege, the communications must be shared between counsel, rather than just between the clients of the joint defense effort.[77]

Finally, information shared between attorneys must further a common *legal* interest. Courts differ in their approaches as to what degree of similarity the legal interest must have in order for the communications to be protected. In *Duplan Corp. v. Deering Milliken, Inc.*, the District of South Carolina stated, "The key consideration is that the nature of the interest be identical, not similar, and be legal, not solely commercial."[78] Other courts adopted this language.[79] However, contrary to this, other courts have relaxed the standard, holding that legal interests must be "demonstrably common" or that the clients must have a "substantial" risk of shared

---

572 (1st Cir. 2001); *see also In re* Teleglobe Commc'ns Corp., 493 F.3d 345, 364 (3d Cir. 2007), *as amended*, Oct. 12, 2007 (adopting the approach of the Restatement (Third) of the Law Governing Lawyers, which notes that joint defense should be referred to as the community-of-interest privilege); *see also* Restatement (Third) of the Law Governing Lawyers § 76 (2000).

71. United States v. Evans, 113 F.3d 1457, 1467 (7th Cir. 1997); Cont'l Oil Co. v. United States, 330 F.2d 347, 350 (9th Cir. 1964).

72. United States v. Schwimmer, 892 F.2d 237, 243 (2d Cir. 1989); *see also* VR Optics, LLC v. Peloton Interactive, LLC, 2019 U.S. Dist. LEXIS 82183 (S.D.N.Y. 2019) (the parties must have "demonstrated cooperation in formulating a common legal strategy" in order to warrant extension of the privilege).

73. *In re* Grand Jury Subpoenas, 89-3 & 89-4, John Doe 89-129, 902 F.2d 244, 248 (4th Cir. 1990); United States v. Gonzalez, 669 F.3d 974, 982 (9th Cir. 2012).

74. W. Fuels Ass'n, Inc. v. Burlington N.R. Co., 102 F.R.D. 201, 203 (D. Wyo. 1984).

75. *In re* Teleglobe Commc'ns Corp., 493 F.3d at 363.

76. MobileMedia Ideas LLC v. Apple Inc., 890 F. Supp. 2d 508, 515 (D. Del. 2012); United States v. Bergonzi, 216 F.R.D. 487, 495 (N.D. Cal. 2003).

77. *In re Teleglobe*, 493 F.3d at 364.

78. Duplan Corp. v. Deering Milliken, Inc., 397 F. Supp. 1146, 1172 (D.S.C. 1974).

79. *See, e.g.*, United States v. Am. Tel. & Tel. Co., 86 F.R.D. 603, 615 (D.D.C. 1979); *see also In re* Pittsburgh Corning Corp., 308 B.R. 716, 728 (Bankr. W.D. Pa. 2004).

exposure to justify sharing privileged information.[80] The Third Circuit in *Teleglobe* backed off *Duplan's* strict identical interest test and stated that "[i]n the community-of-interest context . . . courts can afford to relax the degree to which clients' interests must converge without worrying that their attorneys' ability to represent them zealously and single-mindedly will suffer."[81]

State Medical Peer Review Privileges

The term "medical peer review" refers to the processes by which physicians examine the work or conduct of another physician to determine whether such physician has met accepted standards of care. As the practice of medicine requires extensive, specialized training and knowledge, evaluation of medical decision making is considered to be best undertaken by those with similar knowledge and training, as opposed to evaluation by laypersons or individuals trained in another field.

Where recognized, the peer review privilege generally shields from discovery and prohibits the introduction into evidence of the proceedings and records of medical peer review bodies. The privilege exists to encourage the candid and regular evaluation of physician performance. Such evaluation in turn promotes the delivery of safe, high-quality healthcare and provides mechanisms for addressing performance deficiencies and misconduct. All 50 states and the District of Columbia have some form of peer review privilege.

The Peer Medical Review Privilege in Federal Courts

Although medical malpractice claims, the classic context in which medical peer review materials are sought, arise under state law and are most often filed in state courts, peer review materials may be relevant to, and discoverable in, a number of federal causes of action. These include, but are not limited to, allegations of antitrust violations, employment discrimination, and violations of other federal laws, as well as claims arising under the Federal Tort Claims Act (FTCA). In federal courts, under Federal Rule of Evidence 501, the federal common law—as interpreted by the court in the light of reason and experience—governs a claim of privilege, unless the U.S. Constitution, a federal statute, or rules prescribed by the U.S. Supreme Court provide otherwise. Rule 501 provides that, in a civil case, state law governs privilege regarding a claim or defense for which state law supplies the rule of decision.

Federal privilege rules clearly apply to cases arising under federal antitrust and antidiscrimination laws. Under the FTCA, however, the federal government waives sovereign immunity, subjecting itself to certain tort claims, and

80. SCM Corp. v. Xerox Corp., 70 F.R.D. 508, 525 (D. Conn. 1976); *see also* Am. Legacy Found. v. Lorollard Tobacco Co., No. CIV. A. 19406, 2004 WL 2521289, at *4 (Del. Ch. Nov. 3, 2004) (holding that communications with a substantially similar interest are protected).

81. *In re Teleglobe*, 493 F.3d at 366.

incorporates the substantive law from the state in which the allegedly tortious act or omission occurred. Despite absorbing state substantive law, in nondiversity jurisdiction cases the state law does not supply the rule of decision and, as such, federal privilege law applies.[82] Thus, even if a malpractice or other tort claim based in state law is adjudicated in federal court under the FTCA, federal privilege rules will supplant any state peer review privilege.

Although courts may define and construe privileges by interpreting common-law principles "in the light of reason and experience," courts do not create and apply new federal common-law privileges unless they "promote[ ] sufficiently important interests to outweigh the need for probative evidence."[83] Generally, federal courts have disfavored allowing medical peer review privileges to bar evidence from discovery in antitrust and discrimination suits.[84] Because the allegations in these types of cases often stem from the conduct of individuals participating in the medical peer review process itself, federal courts have reasoned that the medical peer review privilege does not sufficiently promote an interest (e.g., candor on the part of participants) that outweighs the need for probative evidence of violations of federal law.

Recently, the District Court for the Eastern District of Wisconsin extended this reasoning in the context of evidence purportedly protected by the Wisconsin medical peer review privilege, ruling that certain peer review–related materials were discoverable in a case arising out of alleged violations of the federal False Claims Act.[85] The defendants argued that allowing discovery through the use of civil investigative demands under the federal False Claims Act would have a chilling effect on the peer review process. The court recognized that unlike allegations of antitrust violations amounting to misuse of the peer review process, the peer review evidence in this case was not necessary to prove the alleged violations of law. Nevertheless, the government investigation at issue would be hindered by blocking access to the peer review materials. Thus, the court ruled that recognizing the privilege would come at too high a cost and that the defendants could not withhold the peer review materials.[86]

---

82. H.R. Rep. No. 93-1597(1974) (Conf. Rep.), *reprinted in* 1974 U.S.C.C.A.N. 7098, 7101.

83. Jaffee v. Redmond, 518 U.S. 1, 8 (1996) (recognizing a psychotherapist-patient privilege).

84. *See, e.g.,* Adkins v. Christie, 488 F.3d 1324, 1330 (11th Cir. 2007) (racial discrimination action); Virmani v. Novant Health, Inc., 259 F.3d 284, 289 (4th Cir. 2001) (racial discrimination action); Mem'l Hosp. v. Shadur, 664 F.2d 1058, 1063 (7th Cir. 1981) (per curiam) (antitrust action); Zoom Imaging v. St. Luke's Hosp. & Health Network, 513 F. Supp. 2d 411, 415–16 (E.D. Pa. 2007) (antitrust action); Johnson v. Nyack Hosp., 169 F.R.D. 550, 561 (S.D.N.Y. 1996) (racial discrimination action).

85. United States v. Aurora Health Care, Inc., 91 F. Supp. 3d 1066 (E.D. Wis. 2015).

86. *Id.* at 1069; *see also* United States *ex rel.* Polukoff v. St. Mark's Hosp., 2020 U.S. Dist. LEXIS 10154 (D. Utah 2020) (finding that "the vast majority of federal courts addressing the issue [of care review privilege] have declined to adopt a federal care review privilege."). The *Aurora* court also cites a line of cases in which peer review privileges could not be asserted in response to federal subpoenas. *See, e.g., In re* Admin. Subpoena Blue Cross Blue Shield of Mass., Inc., 400 F. Supp. 2d 386, 392–93 (D. Mass. 2015) (administrative investigative subpoena); *In re* Baptist Mem'l Hosp., No. 04-MC-018-DV, 2004 WL 2905391, at *3 (W.D. Tenn. June 22, 2004) (government subpoena following indictment for

In the context of medical malpractice actions arising under the FTCA, the justification for adoption of the peer review privilege under Rule 501 is strongest. Adoption of the privilege encourages candid and regular evaluation of physician performance and in turn higher-quality healthcare. Further, the probative value of the evidence sought to be protected by the privilege is lower than in other types of actions, such as discrimination claims where the conduct of the medical peer review is the subject of the action. Instead, peer review evidence represents only an after-the-fact evaluation of the allegedly tortious action. While it may be relevant, it would rarely be dispositive. Nevertheless, few federal district courts have adopted the privilege.[87] These cases have been characterized as "anomalies in the corpus of federal case law" by at least one court,[88] and defendants asserting the claim should be prepared to argue a fact-specific justification for the application of the privilege under Rule 501 and, moreover, anticipate doing so before a skeptical tribunal.

A number of federal courts have recognized a related "self-critical analysis" privilege.[89] This privilege is predominantly invoked in the healthcare context to protect from discovery the materials generated and information discussed in morbidity and mortality conferences (M&M conferences). M&M conferences are regularly held meetings and occur in many types of healthcare settings (e.g., hospitals, surgery centers, and medical practices). These conferences consist of physician review of complications and errors that occur during patient care and are typically nonpunitive, as the purpose of the conferences is the identification of individual and systemic problems, as well as the promotion of improved care delivery. Courts that have adopted the privilege in this context have generally followed the reasoning of the District Court for the District of Columbia in *Bredice v. Doctors Hosp. Inc.*, where the court stated that "[c]onstructive professional criticism cannot occur in an atmosphere of apprehension that one doctor's suggestion will be used as a denunciation of a colleague's conduct in a malpractice suit" and subjecting these proceedings to the discovery process would likely result in their termination and result in lower-quality medical care.[90]

---

healthcare fraud offenses); Accreditation Ass'n for Ambulatory Health Care, Inc. v. United States, No. 03 C 7380, 2004 WL 783106, at *2–3 (N.D. Ill. Jan. 7, 2004) (administrative subpoena); United States v. United Network for Organ Sharing, No. 02 C 2295, 2002 WL 1726536, at *2 (N.D. Ill. May 17, 2002) (administrative investigative subpoena).

87. *See, e.g.*, Veith v. Portage Cnty., No. 5:11CV2542, 2012 WL 4850197 (N.D. Ohio Oct. 11, 2012); Francis v. United States, No. 09 Civ. 4004, 2011 WL 2224509 (S.D.N.Y. May 31, 2011); KD *ex rel.* Dieffenbach v. United States, 715 F. Supp. 2d 587 (D. Del. 2010).

88. *See* Nilavar v. Mercy Health Sys. W. Ohio, 210 F.R.D. 597, 609 (S.D. Ohio 2002) (reviewing a number of self-critical analysis cases).

89. *See, e.g.*, Bredice v. Doctors Hosp. Inc., 50 F.R.D. 249 (D.D.C. 1970); Weekoty v. United States, 30 F. Supp. 2d 1343 (D.N.M. 1998).

90. *Bredice*, 50 F.R.D. at 250.

The Health Care Quality Improvement Act of 1986

The Health Care Quality Improvement Act (HCQIA)[91] was passed by Congress in response to *Patrick v. Burget*,[92] a case involving a physician's claim that he was subject to allegedly sham peer review proceedings that he contended violated antitrust laws. This case and others in which individual physicians participating as evaluators in medical peer review processes were sued in their individual capacity were perceived to have a chilling effect on the willingness of physicians to participate in medical peer review, because participants feared civil actions as retaliation for their participation. Congress, in recognition of the increasing occurrence of medical malpractice and the need to improve the quality of medical care via peer review, through HCQIA provided qualified immunity from civil damages to participants in "professional review actions." Such immunity extends to the professional review body itself, frequently a committee of a hospital medical staff; any person acting as a member of, or staff to, that body; and any person under contract or other formal agreement with the body, such as a consulting expert.[93]

A professional review action is

> [a]n action or recommendation of a professional review body which is taken or made in the conduct of professional review activity, which is based on the competence or professional conduct of an individual physician (which conduct affects or could affect adversely the health or welfare of a patient or patients), and which affects (or may affect) adversely the clinical privileges, or membership in a professional society, of the physician. Such term includes a formal decision of a professional review body not to take an action or make a recommendation described in the previous sentence and also includes professional review activities relating to a professional review action.[94]

This definition does not, however, include actions primarily based on a physician's association, or lack of association, with a professional society or association; a physician's fees, advertising, or other competitive acts intended to solicit or retain business; a physician's participation in prepaid group health plans, salaried employment, or any other manner of delivering health services, whether on a fee-for-service or other basis; a physician's association with, supervision of, delegation of authority to, support for, training of, or participation in a private group practice with a member or members of a particular class of healthcare practitioner or professional; or any other matters that do not relate to the competence or professional conduct of a physician.[95]

91. 42 U.S.C. § 11101 *et seq.*
92. See 486 U.S. 94 (1988) for the final disposition of the case.
93. 42 U.S.C. § 1111(a)(1).
94. 42 U.S.C. § 11151(9).
95. *Id.*

The definition of a professional review action includes the terms "professional review action" and "professional review body." The term "professional review action" means a healthcare entity's activity with respect to an individual physician to determine whether a physician may have clinical privileges with respect to, or membership in, the entity; to determine the scope of such privileges or membership; or to modify such privileges or membership.[96] The term "professional review body" means a healthcare entity and the governing body or any committee of a healthcare entity that conducts such professional review activities, including any committee of the medical staff of such an entity when assisting the governing body in a professional review activity.[97]

To qualify for immunity under HCQIA, a professional review action must be taken

> [i]n the reasonable belief that the action was in furtherance of quality health care; after a reasonable effort to obtain the facts of the matter; after adequate notice and hearing procedures are afforded to the physician involved or after such other procedures as are fair to the physician under the circumstances; and in the reasonable belief that the action was warranted by the facts known after such reasonable effort to obtain facts and adequate notice and hearing procedures have been afforded to the physician.[98]

HCQIA sets forth carefully prescribed requirements as to the conduct of a professional review action and criteria for a hearing in connection therewith. Failure to meet these requirements can extinguish the immunity provided by HCQIA.

Ostensibly, bad-faith medical peer review is not protected by HCQIA, as such bad-faith actions would not qualify as "being in the furtherance of quality health care" per the statutory mandate. HCQIA does, however, further protect participants in medical peer review by awarding the cost of any plaintiff's suit and reasonable attorney's fees to a prevailing defendant if that defendant has met the standards required of a professional review action and if the plaintiff's claim, or conduct during the litigation of the claim, is found to be frivolous, unreasonable, without foundation, or in bad faith.[99] The specter of paying an opposing party's attorney's fees in some cases may have a chilling effect on challenging, through civil action, the conduct of a professional review action.

Although HCQIA provides qualified immunity from suit to participants in professional review actions on a national basis, it does not establish a nationwide peer review privilege. The confidentiality provisions of HCQIA govern only the transmission of information in connection with the law's reporting requirements, such as the requirement to report adverse actions against physicians and certain

96. *Id.* § 11151(10).
97. *Id.* § 11151(11).
98. *Id.* § 11112(a).
99. *Id.* § 11113.

other licensed healthcare professionals and malpractice payments to the National Practitioner Data Bank. Thus, questions of whether certain documentation or testimony is privileged or inadmissible will be governed by applicable state or federal evidentiary rules.

The Patient Safety and Quality Improvement Act of 2005

The Patient Safety and Quality Improvement Act of 2005 (PSQIA)[100] establishes a voluntary reporting system designed to enhance the data available to assess and resolve patient safety and healthcare quality issues. PSQIA grants the Secretary of the Department of Health and Human Services (HHS) the authority to certify certain entities as "patient safety organizations" to improve patient safety and the quality of healthcare delivery. These entities are overseen by the Agency for Healthcare Research and Quality (AHRQ), which maintains an up-to-date listing of patient safety organizations on its website.[101]

To encourage the reporting and analysis of medical errors, PSQIA privileges and makes confidential certain "patient safety work product." For purposes of PSQIA, patient safety work product means any data, reports, records, memoranda, analyses (such as root cause analyses), and written or oral statements that are assembled and developed for, and reported to, a patient safety organization, or developed by a patient safety organization for the conduct of patient safety activities, or that identify or constitute the deliberations or analysis of, or identify the fact of reporting pursuant to, a patient safety organization's collection, management, or analysis of information.[102]

Such patient safety work product is not subject to subpoena or discovery in any federal, state, or local civil, criminal, administrative, or disciplinary proceeding against a provider and may not be admitted into evidence in any such proceeding.[103] It is further exempt from disclosure under the Freedom of Information Act and any other similar federal or state law and shall otherwise be confidential and not disclosed.[104] There are limited exceptions to the PSQIA privileges, but generally, as long as information qualifies as patient safety work product, it should be protected.[105]

Quality Assurance Privilege

Skilled nursing facilities and nursing facilities (hereinafter referred to as facilities) are institutions that provide skilled nursing care, rehabilitation services, and other

100. *Id.* § 299b-21 *et seq.*
101. *Federally-Listed PSOs*, AHRQ, https://www.pso.ahrq.gov/listed (last visited Oct. 2, 2020).
102. 42 U.S.C. § 299b-21(7).
103. *Id.* § 299b-22(a).
104. *Id.*
105. *See id.* § 299b-22(c).

healthcare services to individuals "who because of their mental or physical condition require care and services above the level of room and board that can only be made available to them through institutional facilities."[106] Pursuant to the Federal Nursing Home Reform Act of 1987, facilities enrolled in the Medicare program must comply with numerous requirements to participate and receive reimbursement from the federal government for care delivered to Medicare beneficiaries. One such requirement involves regular quality assessment and assurance by the facility's quality assessment and assurance committee:

> [Nursing facilities and skilled nursing facilities] must maintain a quality assessment and assurance committee, consisting of the director of nursing services, a physician designated by the facility, and at least 3 other members of the facility's staff, which (i) meets at least quarterly to identify issues with respect to which quality assessment and assurance activities are necessary and (ii) develops and implements appropriate plans of action to correct identified quality deficiencies. [States and the Secretary of HHS and his or her designees] may not require disclosure of the records of such committee, except insofar as such disclosure is related to the compliance with the requirement to maintain such a quality assurance committee.[107]

Courts have interpreted this privilege both narrowly and broadly. In *Boone Retirement Center, Inc. v. Hamilton*, the Supreme Court of Missouri characterized the privilege as "exceedingly narrow," protecting only a quality assurance committee's own records, and that "no honest reading of the statute . . . can extend the [ ] privilege to records and materials generated or created outside the committee and submitted to the committee for its review."[108] In *Jewish Home of Eastern Pennsylvania v. Centers for Medicare and Medicaid Services*, the Third Circuit Court of Appeals held that report forms and witness interview statements given to the Jewish Home's quality assurance committee were not protected by the privilege, as they "were not produced by or at the behest of the quality assurance committee."[109]

However, the Court of Appeals of New York rejected the Missouri Supreme Court's adoption of the narrow approach in *Boone* in *In re Subpoena Duces Tecum to Jane Doe*. The court stated:

> We read the language "records of such committee" as encompassing within its parameters any reports generated by or at the behest of a quality assurance committee for quality assurance purposes . . . compilations, studies or comparisons of clinical data derived from multiple records, created by or at the request of committee personnel for committee use, are "records of such

106. See 42 U.S.C. § 1395i-3(a) for the definition of "skilled nursing facilities" and 42 U.S.C. § 1396r(a) for the definition of "nursing facilities."

107. 42 U.S.C. § 1395i-3(b)(1)(B); 42 U.S.C. § 1396r(b)(1)(B).

108. Boone Ret. Ctr., Inc. v. Hamilton, 946 S.W.2d 740, 743 (Mo. 1997).

109. Jewish Home of E. Pa. v. Ctrs. for Medicare & Medicaid Servs., 693 F.3d 359, 362 (3d Cir. 2012).

committee" and are entitled to protection from disclosure pursuant to federal law.[110]

The Superior Court of Massachusetts took an even broader reading of the statute, considering reports "generally compiled for the purpose of assisting nursing facilities in determining whether certain areas related to patients' quality of care need to be addressed" as protected from discovery, despite not being prepared by, or even at the behest of, a quality assurance committee.[111]

Defendants seeking to preserve this privilege should ensure their strict adherence to the quality assessment and assurance committee standards outlined above, as noncompliance could vitiate the privilege. Whether the privilege will be applied narrowly or broadly depends on the jurisdiction, and as detailed above, jurisdictions vary widely from protecting only those records actually produced by a quality assurance committee to protecting broad swaths of quality assurance materials at the other extreme.

Conclusion

The parameters of the privileges covered in this chapter have developed over time through court decisions and regulatory guidance. The nuances are many, and it can sometimes be difficult to guarantee protection under any given set of circumstances depending on the jurisdiction. However, understanding the scope of the various privileges can minimize the risk of compelled disclosure.

110. Park Assocs. v. N.Y. State Attorney Gen. (*In re* Subpoena Duces Tecum to Jane Doe), 787 N.E.2d 618, 623 (N.Y. 2003).

111. Evans v. Quaboag on the Common, Inc., 26 Mass. L. Rep. 372, at *7 (Mass. Super. Ct. Dec. 7, 2009).

7

THE RECOVERY OF DAMAGES IN HEALTHCARE TORT ACTIONS

Janelle L. Davis and John P. Atkins

Once a plaintiff successfully establishes the defendant's liability for his injuries, the parties must focus on what damages that plaintiff may recover. Damages include economic damages, such as medical expenses, and noneconomic damages, such as pain and suffering, loss of enjoyment of life, and others. This chapter will provide a brief summary of the types of damages available and will discuss various limitations and policy considerations that impact damages awards.

Recovery of Medical Expenses

Plaintiffs will undoubtedly seek the recovery of medical expenses in tort actions. In some jurisdictions, a plaintiff can recover the full amount of the billed medical expenses regardless of whether he actually had to pay any of those expenses out of pocket. An argument can be made that any other result would give the tortfeasor the benefit of the plaintiff's insurance, thereby violating the collateral source rule.[1] Although this can generate a windfall in favor of the patient, the reasoning is that if one party is to receive any sort of benefit or windfall, it should be the injured party who has successfully proven liability.

However, there are states that have rejected this windfall for the injured person. For example, in 2007, the Texas Supreme Court noted that "few patients today ever pay a hospital's full charges, due to the prevalence of Medicare, Medicaid, HMOs, and private insurers who pay discounted rates."[2] In response to this issue, some jurisdictions have enacted so-called "paid or incurred" statutes, and some courts have ruled that a plaintiff may recover only those medical expenses that have actually been paid or incurred by the plaintiff. The applicable statute in Texas is found in section 41.0105 of the Texas Civil Practice and Remedies Code and

1. "Long a part of the common law . . . the [collateral source] rule precludes any reduction in a tortfeasor's liability because of benefits received by the plaintiff from someone else—a collateral source." Haygood v. De Escabedo, 356 S.W.3d 390, 394–95 (Tex. 2011).

2. Daughters of Charity Health Servs. of Waco v. Linnstaedter, 226 S.W.3d 409, 410 (Tex. 2007).

states that the recovery of medical or healthcare expenses is limited to the amount actually paid or incurred by or on behalf of the claimant.[3]

In 2011, the Texas Supreme Court addressed the paid or incurred issue and held that granting damages equal to the total charges billed by the hospital (rather than the reduced amount the insurer paid) would be a windfall. Because the hospital had no claim for these amounts against the patients, the patients in turn had no claim for them against the tortfeasor.[4] The court also held that evidence of medical charges not paid or incurred is irrelevant and likely to generate confusion and is therefore inadmissible in front of the jury.[5] The Texas Supreme Court has continued to construe Texas law this way.[6]

In addition to Texas, other states have specifically addressed the paid or incurred issue. For instance, in 2011 the California Supreme Court considered whether an injured person could recover from the tortfeasor, as economic damages for past medical expenses, the undiscounted sum stated in the medical care provider's bill but never paid by or on behalf of the injured person.[7] The court held that the collateral source rule generally precludes deduction of compensation that the plaintiff received from sources independent of the tortfeasor from damages the plaintiff "would otherwise collect from the tortfeasor."[8] However, the court recognized that this rule has no bearing on amounts that were included in a provider's bill but for which the plaintiff never incurred liability, because the provider, by prior agreement, accepted a lesser amount as full payment.[9] Thus, the plaintiff's damages were reduced to the amount actually paid by her health insurance.[10] In 2012, California attempted to pass S.B. 1528, a bill that would have added to the Civil Code a provision allowing injured persons "to recover the reasonable value

---

3. Tex. Civ. Prac. & Rem. Code § 41.0105 (West 2015).

4. *Haygood*, 356 S.W.3d 390.

5. *Id.* In 2012, a Texas court of appeals reversed and remanded a verdict for the plaintiff after the trial court allowed evidence of the full amount of expenses in front of the jury. The jury awarded the unadjusted amount of medical bills, but after the verdict, the court adjusted the award down to an amount that reflected write-offs and adjustments. Henderson v. Spann, 367 S.W.3d 301 (Tex. App. 2012). Although the trial court adjusted the award after the verdict, the court of appeals still reversed because allowing evidence of the full amount of the bills was reversible error. Since the plaintiff was not entitled to recover the unadjusted amount of medical bills, the jury was not entitled to hear evidence of it.

6. *See* Gunn v. McCoy, 554 S.W.3d 645, 672 (Tex. 2018), *reh'g denied* (Sept. 28, 2018).

7. Howell v. Hamilton Meats & Provisions, Inc., 257 P.3d 1130 (Cal. 2011).

8. *Id.* at 1135.

9. *Id.*

10. *Id.* Following this 2011 decision, in 2012 a California court of appeals held that "where an employer is required under the workers' compensation laws to pay in full an injured employee's medical expenses, the injured employee may not recover, as economic damages from a third party tortfeasor, medical fees that the provider is precluded either by agreement or by law (including the statutory fee schedule), from collecting from the employer." Sanchez v. Brooke, 204 Cal. App. 4th 126, 142 (Ct. App. 2012).

of medical services provided without regard to the amount actually paid." The law ultimately failed to pass.[11]

The Kansas Supreme Court has held that evidence of the amount actually paid for medical services was relevant to the question of the reasonable value of those services and could therefore be admitted despite the collateral source rule.[12] The court based its opinion largely upon the reasoning of several other state high courts, including pre-*Howell* California precedent.

Some states have proved more resistant to changes in the traditional collateral source rule. For example, in Colorado, an injured plaintiff may recover the amount billed, and the defendant is barred from presenting evidence of the lower amount that the healthcare provider accepted to satisfy the bill.[13] Similarly, the Supreme Court of West Virginia has held that the collateral source rule continues to exclude evidence of contractual discounts where medical damages are concerned.[14]

Louisiana has taken its own unique approach. Reasoning that a plaintiff is not entitled to the benefit of write-offs that the plaintiff did not pay consideration for, the Louisiana Supreme Court reasoned in a pair of opinions that plaintiffs are not entitled to recover the portions of their medical expenses written off by the provider if they are covered by Medicaid or workers' compensation.[15] In October 2015, the Louisiana Supreme Court took this one step further, finding that where a plaintiff's lawyer had negotiated a discount in medical expenses, the plaintiff could not recover the amount written off because he did not actually "incur" those expenses.[16]

In New York, at least one court applied the state's collateral source rule to require a postverdict setoff of the difference between the amount billed and the amount paid.[17] Pennsylvania courts follow the same approach as Texas: Only

11. *Howell* remains good law in California, and it does not appear that any overruling statute has been adopted. *See, e.g.*, Libman v. S. Wine & Spirits of Am., Inc., No. B287345, 2019 WL 6871781, at *9 (Cal. Ct. App. Dec. 17, 2019).

12. Martinez v. Milburn Enters., Inc., 233 P.3d 205, 228 (Kan. 2010).

13. Volunteers of Am. v. Gardenswartz, 242 P.3d 1080 (Colo. 2010). This decision is based in part on the Colorado Supreme Court's construction of a contractual savings clause in a Colorado statute intended to limit double recoveries. The court reasons that insurance discounts are one of the benefits contracted for, and consequently they arise from a collateral source. *See id. Gardenswartz* remains the Colorado Supreme Court's most recent pronouncement on this question.

14. Kenney v. Liston, 760 S.E.2d 434, 446 (W. Va. 2014) (holding, at substantial length, that under West Virginia law, the collateral source rule, as traditionally conceived, still applies, even to medical costs).

15. Bozeman v. State, 879 So. 2d 692, 705 (La. 2004) (Medicaid); Benoit v. Turner Indus. Grp., L.L.C., 85 So. 3d 629, 635 (La. 2012) (workers' compensation).

16. Hoffman v. 21st Century N. Am. Ins. Co., No. 2014–C–2279, 2015 WL 5776131 (La. Oct. 2, 2015).

17. Kastick v. U-Haul Co. of W. Mich., 740 N.Y.S.2d 167 (App. Div. 2002). Although this case is older, it continues to be favorably cited as authoritative regarding New York law. *See, e.g.*, Bauta v. Greyhound Lines, Inc., 14-CV-3725 (RER), 2018 WL 10466841, at *1 (E.D.N.Y. July 2, 2018); Kihl v. Pfeffer, 47 A.D.3d 154, 163 (N.Y. 2007). Note that in New York, collateral source common law is

evidence of the amount paid is relevant.[18] In Ohio, discounted medical bills are not encompassed by the collateral source rule. Thus, the jury may consider both the amount billed and the amount paid in determining the "reasonable value" of the medical services.[19]

These changes to the collateral source rule are not without their own unintended policy consequences. For instance, a tort victim might refuse to submit her bills to his health insurer in an effort to "incur" more medical expenses for purposes of a lawsuit or settlement. Such a strategy raises policy and possibly even ethical concerns. An adverse party might argue that this represents a failure to mitigate damages. Practitioners should pay careful attention to the rules in their respective states to make certain they are presenting the best admissible evidence establishing their position on the reasonable cost of medical services.

Noneconomic Damages

Noneconomic damages include categories of damages that are often controversial. In particular, noneconomic damages include recovery for pain and suffering, loss of enjoyment of life, loss of companionship or consortium, and disfigurement, among others. These types of damages are controversial because there is no clear way to measure them. Medical expenses are comparatively straightforward because they can be proven with medical bills or receipts (though, as described above, whether they are reasonable is a question that may not be simple). But with noneconomic damages, who is to say how much the loss of enjoyment of someone's life is worth? Does it depend on how much the plaintiff "enjoyed" his life before he was injured? How is a jury supposed to put a dollar figure on someone's pain and suffering?

Noneconomic damages are also somewhat sensitive because they have the tendency to appeal to the emotions of the jury and are the most likely candidate for causing a large jury verdict. For this reason, many states have vigorously pursued and enacted tort reform laws that place limits on the amount of recovery for noneconomic damages. Although this topic has been discussed in Chapter 5, below is a short summary of the caps applicable in each state.[20]

---

overwritten by a statute designed to reduce double recoveries, which is analyzed by modern case law on the subject.

18. Moorehead v. Crozer Chester Med. Ctr., 765 A.2d 786 (Pa. 2001). This case was partially overruled in 2008 with respect to the proposition that a stipulation cannot preclude a legal analysis of damages due—however, it does not appear that *Moorehead*'s analysis of what constitutes the "reasonable value of medical services" was overturned. *See* Northbrook Life Ins. Co. v. Commw., 949 A.2d 333, 337 (Pa. 2008); Hilburn v. Enerpipe Ltd., 442 P.3d 509, 524 (Kan. 2019) (overturning as unconstitutional Kansas damages cap that the court had previously held constitutional).

19. Robinson v. Bates, 857 N.E.2d 1195 (Ohio 2006).

20. States not listed below do not have clear caps on damages. They may have limitations based on due process principles. For instance, Arizona constitutionally prohibits laws limiting the amount of damages in personal injury and wrongful death actions but also applies due process to prohibit excessive awards. ARIZ. CONST. art. II, § 31; Sec. Title Agency, Inc. v. Pope, 200 P.3d 977, 1001 (Ariz. Ct.

- **Alabama:** $400,000 cap on noneconomic damages in medical malpractice cases only.[21]
- **Alaska:** $400,000 cap in all tort cases (or life expectancy × $8,000).[22] If the person experiences permanent physical impairment or severe disfigurement, then the damages may not exceed the greater of $1,000,000 or the person's life expectancy × $25,000.[23]
- **California:** Statutory cap of $250,000, only for medical malpractice.[24]
- **Colorado:** $500,000 cap in all tort actions except medical malpractice; $250,000 in medical malpractice actions before July 1, 2003, $300,000 thereafter.[25]
- **Florida:** Previous cap of $450,000 was held unconstitutional in 1986.[26] New caps apply only in medical malpractice cases, and their constitutionality has not yet been determined.
- **Hawaii:** $375,000. The exceptions to this cap include victims of intentional torts, environmental pollution, toxic and asbestos-related injuries, strict and products liability torts, aircraft accidents, and motor vehicle accidents.[27]
- **Idaho:** $250,000 cap adjusted by industrial commission adjustment in average annual wage, starting July 1, 2004.[28]
- **Indiana:** Current cap of $1,800,000 on noneconomic damages in medical malpractice actions only.[29]
- **Louisiana:** $500,000 cap for medical malpractice.[30]

App. 2008). In other cases, previously extant liability limitations have been ruled unconstitutional, for instance in Illinois, Kansas, and Oklahoma. *See* Lebron v. Gottlieb Mem'l Hosp., 930 N.E.2d 895, 914 (Ill. 2010) (Illinois); Hilburn v. Enerpipe Ltd., 442 P.3d 509, 514 (Kan. 2019) (Kansas); Beason v. I.E. Miller Servs., Inc., 441 P.3d 1107, 1109 (Okla. 2019) (Oklahoma).

21. Ala. Code § 6-5-44 (1975). This cap was held unconstitutional in 1991. Moore v. Mobile Infirmary Ass'n, 592 So. 2d 156 (Ala. 1991).

22. Alaska Stat. § 09.17.010.

23. *Id.*

24. Cal. Civ. Code § 3333.2. This has been held constitutional. Fein v. Permanente Med. Grp., 695 P.2d 665 (Cal. 1985).

25. Colorado statute provides, in pertinent part: "In any civil action other than medical malpractice actions in which damages for noneconomic loss or injury may be awarded, the total of such damages shall not exceed the sum of two hundred fifty thousand dollars, unless the court finds justification by clear and convincing evidence therefor. In no case shall the amount of noneconomic loss or injury damages exceed five hundred thousand dollars." Colo. Rev. Stat. Ann. § 13-21-102.5 (West 2015). This statute was held constitutional in 2004. Garhart *ex rel.* Tinsman v. Columbia/Healthone, L.L.C., 95 P.3d 571, 581 (Colo. 2004). For medical malpractice cases, Colorado statute initially provided for a maximum noneconomic recovery of $250,000, but this was adjusted to $300,000 for inflation. Colo. Rev. Stat. Ann. § 13-64-302 (West 2015).

26. Smith v. Dep't of Ins., 507 So. 2d 1080 (Fla. 1987).

27. Haw. Rev. Stat. §§ 663-8.5, 663-8.7, 663-10.9(2).

28. Idaho Code Ann. §§ 6-1603, 72-409(2).

29. Ind. Code § 34-18-14-3.

30. La. Rev. Stat. Ann. § 40:1299.42.

- **Maine:** $750,000 cap in wrongful death actions, with $250,000 punitive damages cap.[31]
- **Maryland:** $500,000 cap in personal injury and wrongful death actions. The cap has been increasing by $15,000 every year since 1995. In a wrongful death action involving two or more claimants, total noneconomic damages award may not exceed 150 percent of the base cap.[32]
- **Massachusetts:** $500,000 cap in medical malpractice cases.[33]
- **Michigan:** $280,000 cap in medical malpractice cases, except under certain enumerated exceptions, in which case cap is $500,000.[34]
- **Mississippi:** $1,000,000 cap. Constitutionally ambiguous under existing precedent.[35]
- **Missouri:** Cap on noneconomic damages in medical malpractice cases removed in 2012.
- **Montana:** No statutory limit on damages, but government panel reviews medical malpractice cases and may recommend an award.[36]
- **Nebraska:** Medical malpractice cap against provider of $2,250,000.[37]
- **Nevada:** $350,000 cap in medical malpractice cases.[38]
- **New Mexico:** $600,000 cap in medical malpractice cases only.[39]
- **North Carolina:** $500,000 cap beginning in 2011, adjusted every three years by changes in consumer price index, in medical malpractice cases.[40]
- **North Dakota:** $500,000 cap in medical malpractice cases.[41]
- **Ohio:** The cap applies in tort actions and provides a sliding scale between $250,000 and $500,000 depending on size of economic damages and number of plaintiffs. There is a maximum of $500,000 for any single occurrence, unless there is a severe injury such as a deformity or loss of limb or a permanent physical function injury that deprives the injured person of her independence, in which case the maximum is increased to $500,000 per plaintiff, or $1,000,000 per occurrence.[42]

---

31. Me. Rev. Stat. tit. 18-C, § 2-807.
32. Md. Code Ann., Cts. & Jud. Proc. § 11-108; John Crane, Inc. v. Scribner, 800 A.2d 727 (Md. 2002).
33. Mass. Gen. Laws Ann. ch. 231, § 60H.
34. Mich. Comp. Laws § 600.1483.
35. Miss. Code Ann. § 11-1-60. One circuit court has held the cap unconstitutional. Tanner v. Eagle Oil & Gas Co., 2012 WL 7748580 (Miss. Cir.). The Mississippi Supreme Court has punted on the question. *See* Sears, Roebuck & Co. v. Learmonth, 95 So. 3d 633, 637 (Miss. 2012) (declining to address the issue, since the court was presented with a $4 million general verdict, and it was possible that the noneconomic portion was less than $1,000,000).
36. Mont. Code Ann. §§ 27-6-606(2), 27-6-701.
37. Neb. Rev. Stat. § 44-2825(1).
38. Nev. Rev. Stat. § 41A.035.
39. N.M. Stat. Ann. § 41-5-6.
40. N.C. Gen. Stat. § 90-21.19.
41. N.D. Cent. Code § 32-42-02.
42. Ohio Rev. Code Ann. § 2323.43.

- **Oregon:** $500,000 cap in bodily injury, death, or property damage actions. The cap has been held unconstitutional in personal injury actions but constitutional in wrongful death cases or other actions not recognized at common law.[43]
- **South Carolina:** Inflation-adjusted medical malpractice cap.[44]
- **South Dakota:** $500,000 cap on general damages in medical malpractice cases, no limits on special damages.[45]
- **Tennessee:** $750,000 cap with certain exceptions.[46]
- **Texas:** $250,000 or $500,000 medical malpractice cap depending on number of liable providers.[47]
- **Utah:** Currently $450,000 adjusted cap for medical malpractice.[48] Ruled unconstitutional as applied to wrongful death cases.[49]
- **Virginia:** Medical malpractice cap that adjusts each year until 2031, currently $2.45 million.[50]
- **West Virginia:** $500,000 cap on noneconomic loss adjusted by inflation, except that if the healthcare professional does not have the required insurance, no limit applies.[51]
- **Wisconsin:** Annually adjusted cap for medical malpractice cases.[52]

As noted above, the states not listed do not presently have effective caps on noneconomic damages in healthcare-related tort cases.

Constitutionality of State Law Caps on Noneconomic Damages

State law caps on the recovery of noneconomic damages are not without controversy. In fact, the majority of them have been challenged on constitutional grounds. In some instances, these challenges have been successful. However, there are competing concerns at play when it comes to caps on noneconomic damages. For example, there is a need for the state to balance its desire to create a positive business climate with its desire to fairly compensate tort victims. In addition, the availability of insurance coverage further complicates the issue. Because of these

43. OR. REV. STAT. ANN. § 31.710; Klutschkowski v. Peacehealth, 311 P.3d 461 (Or. 2013).
44. S.C. CODE ANN. § 15-32-220.
45. S.D. CODIFIED LAWS § 21-3-11.
46. TENN. CODE ANN. § 29-39-102. Exceptions include cases involving catastrophic injuries, intentional conduct, intentional destruction or falsification of records, alcohol or drug influence, or if the defendant's wrongful act results in defendant being convicted of a felony. *Id.*
47. TEX. CIV. PRAC. & REM. CODE ANN. § 74.301.
48. UTAH CODE ANN. § 78B-3-410.
49. Smith v. United States, 356 P.3d 1249, 1258 (Utah 2015).
50. VA. CODE ANN. § 8.01-581.15.
51. W. VA. CODE § 55-7B-8.
52. WIS. STAT. §§ 655.017, 893.55(4)(d).

competing concerns, caps on noneconomic damages have been upheld in a number of states.

Those who argue that the caps are not constitutional typically raise one or more of eight main arguments. First, they argue that statutory caps violate the right to a jury trial by usurping the jury's role in awarding damages. Second, they argue the related point that a cap on the amount of noneconomic damages circumvents the constitutional amendment process as it relates to the right to a jury trial. Third, opponents argue that the caps violate the separation of powers by giving a state's legislature the right to limit the effect of a court judgment. Fourth, they argue that caps violate the principle of uniform operation of the law. Specifically, in one state, this argument has been used to claim that the caps discriminate against victims with significant quality-of-life damages. Fifth, opponents argue that statutory caps on damages violate the prohibition against special legislation because they confer a special benefit to the exclusion of others. Sixth, some argue that the caps are an unconstitutional form of legislative remittitur. The seventh argument against the constitutionality of caps on noneconomic damages is that they violate the due process rights of plaintiffs and/or the equal protection clause. And finally, opponents sometimes argue that statutory caps violate the open courts doctrine.

Of course, for all the arguments against the constitutionality of statutory caps on noneconomic damages, there are arguments for their constitutionality. These arguments fall under four main categories. First, proponents argue that the caps do not violate the open courts doctrine because plaintiffs still have an available remedy through the courts. In other words, the caps do not take away all damages awarded by a jury. Second, the caps do not violate the equal protection clause because even if there is "discrimination" against tort victims, it is not discrimination in an unconstitutional sense. The legislature is merely trying to reduce the costs for business and, in a medical malpractice context, the healthcare costs for individuals. The third argument supporting the constitutionality of statutory caps is that they do not violate due process because there is a rational basis for them, i.e., reducing costs for businesses. Fourth, proponents of statutory caps argue that they do not unconstitutionally violate the separation of powers because they are simply an expression of the law to be applied.

The previous section cites several of the cases interpreting the constitutionality of various damages limitations, including several fairly recent decisions striking down such limitations. These cases show the various constitutional arguments at play.

Medical Monitoring

In recent years a new remedy, known as medical monitoring, has emerged. This remedy compensates plaintiffs for medical expenses that they incur over time in periodically monitoring their health for conditions that may develop as a result of the defendant's conduct. This remedy seems to be in direct conflict with the general rule that medical expenses are recoverable when an immediate, recognizable injury is present. However, an increasing number of states have started recognizing medical monitoring as an appropriate remedy.

In states that do recognize the remedy without requiring a present injury to the plaintiff, the plaintiff is required to prove the following elements: significant exposure to a proven toxic or hazardous substance because of the defendant's tortious conduct; as a result of the exposure, a significantly increased risk of contracting a serious disease, illness, or injury; a medical test for early detection of the injury exists and is beneficial; and periodic monitoring and testing have been prescribed by a physician as reasonably necessary.[53] Although these claims most often arise in the environmental or toxic tort context, they have been recognized in prescription drug and medical device cases.[54] For example, in Kentucky, plaintiffs who used the diet drug fen-phen alleged a significant increase in their risk of serious injury and disease as a result of consuming the drug.[55] The court ultimately dismissed the claim because the plaintiffs did not show a present physical injury, but the court recognized that this particular type of case would be appropriate for a medical monitoring claim.[56]

Loss of Companionship or Consortium

Damages for loss of companionship or consortium typically arise in wrongful death cases. Technically, however, loss of consortium is the appropriate measure of damages for any deprivation of the benefits of a family relationship due to the actions of a tortfeasor.[57] Some states, like Georgia,[58] Louisiana,[59] and Maine,[60] treat loss of consortium as a separate cause of action, while other states treat it as a type of damages.[61]

For those states that treat loss of consortium as a form of damages, whether the damages may be properly characterized as economic or noneconomic depends on the state and what the state construes "loss of consortium" to mean. Maryland,

53. *See, e.g.,* Donovan v. Philip Morris USA, Inc., 455 Mass. 215, 226 (2009); Hansen v. Mountain Fuel Supply Co., 858 P.2d 970, 979 (Utah 1993); Ayers v. Twp. of Jackson, 106 N.J. 557, 605–06 (1987); *In re* Paoli R.R. Yard PCB Litig., 916 F.2d 829, 852 (3d Cir. 1990).

54. *See, e.g.,* Sinclair v. Merck & Co., Inc., 195 N.J. 51 (2008) (seeking damages for medical monitoring after use of prescription drug Vioxx); Wood v. Wyeth-Ayerst Labs., Div. of Am. Home Prods., 82 S.W.3d 849 (Ky. 2002) (fen-phen).

55. *Wood*, 82 S.W.3d at 850–51.

56. *Id.* at 854–55. Other states have considered and rejected medical monitoring claims in the absence of a physical injury. *See* Caronia v. Philip Morris USA, Inc., 5 N.E.3d 11, 14 (N.Y. 2013) (answering certified question from the Second Circuit and answering in the negative in part due to lack of physical injury).

57. *See, e.g.,* Smith v. Clement, 797 So. 2d 151, 158 (La. App. 3 Cir. 2001) (discussing elements of damages in a loss of consortium claim).

58. *See* White v. Hubbard, 416 S.E.2d 568 (Ga. App. 1992).

59. *See* Ferrell v. Fireman's Fund Ins. Co., 696 So. 2d 569 (La. 1997).

60. ME. REV. STAT. tit. 14, § 302.

61. Ohio's rule regarding loss of consortium in wrongful death cases is a typical example. *See, e.g.,* OHIO REV. CODE ANN. § 2125.02.

for instance, considers loss of consortium damages to be nonpecuniary and thus noneconomic and therefore subject to Maryland's noneconomic damages cap.[62] In other states, loss of consortium is subject to a broader definition and will include not only loss of comfort and society (the family relationship) but also loss of service—the reasonable value of the injured or deceased family member's contributions in money.[63] Although the loss of comfort and society is a form of noneconomic damages, loss of service is obviously economic in nature.

Therefore, in deciding questions like the applicability of limitations on noneconomic damages to loss of consortium, it is vitally important for an attorney to carefully research the elements of loss of consortium damages under state law. This is especially true given that much of the legal authority on loss of consortium arises out of state common law, ensuring that there is (and probably always will be) a great deal of variation among states with respect to how loss of consortium damages are treated.

Punitive Damages

Punitive (sometimes called "exemplary") damages are distinct from other forms of noneconomic damages. The foregoing categories of noneconomic damages and economic damages have in common that their goal is ultimately compensation—to put the plaintiff back in the position she would have been in but for defendant's actions. Punitive damages, by contrast, are not compensatory in nature. Instead, the goal of punitive damages is to exact an economic penalty that will deter future malfeasance by the party being punished.[64]

Because punitive damages are calibrated to punish and deter, rather than to compensate, proof of harm is insufficient to support punitive damages. Instead, a plaintiff must prove both harm and a particularly culpable mental state. For instance, in the states of Alabama,[65] Connecticut,[66] Oklahoma,[67] and Texas,[68] the plaintiff must show that the defendant acted with a mental state like reckless disregard, oppression, fraud, wantonness, malice, or gross negligence. In many jurisdictions, like Alabama,[69] the District of Columbia,[70] South Dakota,[71] and Texas,[72] this burden is heightened by the additional requirement that the culpable mental state be proved by clear and convincing evidence.

62. Md. Code Ann., Cts. & Jud. Proc. § 11-108.
63. Payne v. Eighth Jud. Dist. Ct., 60 P.3d 469 (Mont. 2002).
64. *See, e.g.*, Exxon Shipping Co. v. Baker, 554 U.S. 471 (2008).
65. Ala. Code § 6-11-20.
66. Champagne v. Raybestos-Manhattan, Inc., 562 A.2d 1100 (Conn. 1989).
67. Okla. Stat. tit. 23, § 9.1.
68. Tex. Civ. Prac. & Rem. Code Ann. § 41.003.
69. Ala. Code § 6-11-20.
70. Jonathan Woodner Co. v. Breeden, 665 A.2d 929 (D.C. 1995).
71. S.D. Codified Laws § 21-1-4.1.
72. Tex. Civ. Prac. & Rem. Code Ann. § 41.003.

Further complicating the state-by-state picture, some states, like Ohio,[73] New Hampshire,[74] and South Dakota,[75] further limit the availability of punitive damages only to certain types of action, either by listing the claims eligible for punitive damages in statute or by excluding punitive damages for certain types of claims by court decision. And some jurisdictions do not permit punitive damages at all.[76]

After determining that punitive damages are available in a particular case, the next question is how large the award can be. Some states have placed limits on the amount of recoverable punitive damages. These limits are often based on some proportion of the amount of compensatory damages awarded by the trier of fact.

Even those states that cap punitive damages, however, do not all do it in the same way. In Alabama, punitive damages in personal injury actions are generally limited to three times compensatory damages or $1,500,000, whichever is greater.[77] In Alaska, a punitive damages award may not exceed $500,000 or three times the compensatory damages awarded by the trier of fact, whichever is greater.[78] Mississippi caps punitive damages based on a sliding scale depending on the net worth of the defendant. This cap does not apply, however, if the defendant was convicted of a felony that caused the injury or if the defendant was under the influence of drugs or alcohol at the time of the injury.[79] North Carolina limits punitive damages to $250,000 or three times the economic damages awarded by the trier of fact, whichever is greater.[80] North Dakota limits them to $250,000 or double economic damages, whichever is greater.[81]

In addition to the various state law limits on punitive damages, the Supreme Court of the United States has determined that certain punitive damage awards can be so excessive as to violate the due process guarantee of the Fourteenth Amendment. In *BMW of North America, Inc. v. Gore* in 1996, the Court held that a grossly excessive award of punitive damages violates due process and enunciated a three-factor test (reprehensibility of the defendant's conduct, ratio of compensatory to punitive damages, and sanctions for comparable misconduct) for determining whether a particular award is excessive.[82] In *Cooper Industries, Inc. v. Leatherman Tool Group, Inc.*, in 2001, the Court ruled that the appropriate standard of review for lower court determinations of the constitutionality of a punitive

73. Robeck v. Ohio, 374 N.E.2d 411 (Ohio 1978) (no punitive damages in wrongful death suits).

74. N.H. Rev. Stat. Ann. § 507:16.

75. S.D. Codified Laws § 21-1-4.

76. "The law of Puerto Rico does not, as a general rule, recognize or permit the recovery of punitive damages." NPR, Inc. v. Am. Int'l Ins. Co. of P.R., 242 F. Supp. 2d 121, 127 (D.P.R. 2003).

77. Ala. Code § 6-11-21(j).

78. Alaska Stat. § 09.17.020(f). Alaska raises the limit to the greatest of four times compensatory damages, four times the improper financial gain, or $7,000,000 if the conduct was motivated by financial gain or if the adverse consequences were actually known by the defendant or the person responsible for making policy decisions on behalf of the defendant. *Id.* at § 09.17.020(g).

79. Miss. Code Ann. § 11-1-65(3).

80. N.C. Gen. Stat. § 1D-25.

81. N.D. Cent. Code § 32-03.2-11.

82. BMW of N. Am., Inc. v. Gore, 517 U.S. 559, 562, 574–85 (1996).

damages award is de novo, rather than the more deferential standard of abuse of discretion.[83]

The Court provided clearer substantive guidance in 2003 in *State Farm Mutual Automobile Insurance Co. v. Campbell,* explaining that in general a punitive damages award will comport with due process when the ratio of the punitive award to the compensatory award is a single digit (2:1, 3:1, 4:1, etc.); however, the Court hedged and noted that in cases involving particularly egregious conduct, this guideline might be exceeded.[84] Four years later, in 2007, the Supreme Court held in *Philip Morris USA v. Williams* that a trier of fact may not consider harm caused by the defendant's conduct to persons other than those who are parties to the suit when determining the size of a punitive damages award.[85] Applying the law it made in the foregoing cases, especially the factor analysis from *State Farm Mutual,* the Supreme Court held in 2008 that the ratio of punitive damages to compensatory damages should not exceed 1:1 in cases arising under maritime law.[86]

An attorney considering the rules applicable to punitive damages in a particular case has a lot to think about: not only must she determine, based on state law, whether such an award is available, she must also consider what mental state is required, whether that mental state must be proved under a heightened standard of proof, and whether a damages cap applies. After all that, an award can still be struck down as "grossly excessive" under federal constitutional principles.

Comparative and Contributory Negligence

Obviously, an important question impacting damages in any kind of negligence case is the proportional responsibility of all the involved parties. While a few states still cling to the traditional contributory negligence rule that any negligence on the part of the plaintiff forecloses recovery,[87] most states have adopted one of two comparative negligence frameworks.

The first of these frameworks is "pure" comparative negligence (or comparative fault), in which a party's share of damages will be exactly proportional to the amount the party's negligence contributed to the injury. For instance, in a case with one plaintiff and two defendants, if a jury finds that each is one-third at fault, each defendant will pay one-third of the total damages plaintiff suffered, and the plaintiff will not receive compensation for the one-third of his damages attributable

83. Cooper Indus., Inc. v. Leatherman Tool Grp., Inc., 532 U.S. 424, 436 (2001).

84. State Farm Mut. Auto. Ins. Co. v. Campbell, 538 U.S. 408, 425 (2003).

85. Philip Morris USA v. Williams, 549 U.S. 346, 355 (2007).

86. Exxon Shipping Co. v. Baker, 554 U.S. 471, 514 (2008).

87. For instance, Alabama still holds to the traditional contributory negligence rule. *See* John Cowley & Bros., Inc. v. Brown, 569 So. 2d 375 (Ala. 1990). So does Maryland. Bd. of Cnty. Comm'r of Garrett Cnty. v. Bell Atlantic, 695 A.2d 171 (Md. 1997).

to his own negligence. Examples of pure comparative negligence states include Alaska,[88] California,[89] and Mississippi.[90]

The most common negligence rule is called "partial" or "modified" comparative negligence (or comparative fault). Under this rule, damages are generally assessed and liability spread just as they would be in a pure comparative negligence jurisdiction. However, if the trier of fact determines that a plaintiff's share of responsibility is half or more (in some states) or greater than half (in other states), the plaintiff will recover *nothing*. Most states appear to believe that the partial comparative negligence rule best splits the difference between contributory negligence and pure comparative negligence. States that bar recovery if *half or more* of the plaintiff's damages are attributable to his own negligence include Arkansas,[91] Colorado,[92] and Nebraska.[93] States that bar recovery if *greater than half* of plaintiff's damages are attributable to his own negligence include Hawaii,[94] Indiana,[95] South Carolina,[96] and Texas.[97]

Conclusion

Given that even the best liability case is not worth much if damages did not result, a savvy practitioner includes a damages analysis in any presuit investigation. The available damages will be driven both by the actual loss suffered by the plaintiff and by the local laws stating what portion of those damages can legally be recovered.

88. Alaska Stat. §§ 09.17.060, 09.17.080.
89. Diaz v. Carcamo, 253 P.3d 535 (Cal. 2011).
90. Miss. Code Ann. § 11-7-15.
91. Ark. Code Ann. § 16-64-122.
92. B.G.'s, Inc. v. Gross, 23 P.3d 691 (Colo. 2001).
93. Neb. Rev. Stat. §§ 25-21, 185.11.
94. Haw. Rev. Stat. § 663-31.
95. Ind. Code § 34-51-2-6 (claimant's recovery barred if claimant's fault "is greater than the fault of all persons whose fault proximately contributed to the claimant's damages").
96. Ross v. Paddy, 532 S.E.2d 612 (S.C. Ct. App. 2000) (plaintiff may recover if "his or her negligence is not greater" than defendant's).
97. Tex. Civ. Prac. & Rem. Code Ann. § 33.001 (using the phrase "greater than 50 percent").

8

EXPERTS

Kimberly Grant Silvus

Expert witnesses are at the heart of a healthcare liability or medical malpractice action. Courts in the United States rely heavily on the opinion testimony of healthcare providers to educate judges and juries on the medical complexities of a case. Expert witnesses identify and explain standards of care and practices that are compliant with or in deviation from those standards, identify and explain injuries sustained by patients as well as the likely causes of those injuries, and offer opinions about a patient's future prognosis and medical needs. Without the opinion testimony of the expert witnesses in a medical malpractice case, juries would not have any information from which they could distinguish injuries caused by wrongdoing of the defendant provider from injuries that are simply caused by acceptable risks associated with a given treatment.

Finding the right experts for a case and understanding how to make the most of their opinions are a critical aspect of the pursuit or defense of a medical malpractice lawsuit. For those attorneys who have stayed far away from biology, chemistry, and anatomy and who certainly did not go to medical school, trying to navigate the expert witness aspect of a medical malpractice case can be daunting and intimidating. A lawyer is suddenly supposed to draw on a liberal arts degree in literature or history and look at an injured person, identify the specialty of medicine responsible for the injury, spar in some intelligible meaningful manner with experts on the other side in a deposition, confidently present her experts at trial, spar again with the experts for the other side—this time with an audience—and then distill the immensely complicated medicine into a persuasive comprehensible narrative for a jury. And lawyers must accomplish this within the confines of procedural and evidentiary rules governing who qualifies as an expert, what type of information must be disclosed to the other side, and in which circumstances and by what means a lawyer can challenge the admissibility of an expert or her specific opinions.

The procedural and evidentiary rules involved in the expert witness aspect of a medical malpractice case require careful thought and analysis. This chapter will provide a basic introduction to this challenging phase of a healthcare lawsuit. After a brief introduction to the role of experts in healthcare liability actions, this chapter will address generally how to decide on the type of expert, how to obtain the expert, and the requisite contents of a Rule 26 disclosure. It will then address the issue of deciding whether a treating healthcare provider constitutes an expert witness and discuss the means by which a party can challenge the admissibility of an expert or portions of her opinions at trial.

The Role of an Expert

With limited exceptions, a plaintiff cannot establish his prima facie case for medical malpractice without experts, and a defendant would face a significant uphill battle without them. A plaintiff has the burden of establishing a prima facie case that the medical provider in question deviated from the applicable standard of care and that the deviation caused a harm to the patient that otherwise would not have occurred. With certain exceptions, the plaintiff meets this burden by introducing the testimony of qualified expert witnesses. The plaintiff's expert witnesses must be disclosed to the defendant in advance of trial, and the requisite content of these disclosures in federal court is controlled by Rule 26 of the Federal Rules of Civil Procedure.[1] Similarly, any expert witness a defendant intends to present at trial must be disclosed to the plaintiff in advance of trial. No witness may offer opinion testimony at trial if that witness has not been disclosed to the other side in advance of trial in compliance with the Rules of Civil Procedure.

The expert witness component of a medical malpractice case raises several questions, but the initial ones are how to decide what type of expert is needed and what is required by the Rules of Civil Procedure in an expert disclosure. Beyond these two basic questions are more nuanced issues of who constitutes an expert that must be disclosed in advance of trial, who is qualified to be an expert, and under what circumstances and by what mechanism can one side challenge the admissibility of a disclosed expert's opinions. Questions often arise concerning whether treating healthcare providers of the plaintiff are expert witnesses for whom a disclosure is required. This chapter strives to provide basic guidance and suggestions on these issues.

Determining the Type of Expert Needed

Both plaintiff and defendant need at least one expert (and likely more than one) in a medical malpractice case, given the complexities inherent in such cases. At the most basic level, the case will typically involve issues of standard of care, causation, and injury or damages. Acquiring reviewing or consulting experts early in the course of litigation is advisable, because as the case develops, other medical issues could arise where expert opinion from a very specific specialty may be helpful. Often a case will have a deadline by which each side must disclose expert witnesses.

1. Please see the relevant state court rules of procedure for the applicable parallel rule.

Standard of Care

First, identify the type of medicine practiced by the defendant provider. The logical starting place for finding an initial consulting expert would be with a healthcare provider who practices the same specialty as the defendant provider. If there is only one healthcare provider whose care is at issue in the lawsuit, this can be relatively simple. For example, if the medical issue in the case is the manner in which an orthopedic surgeon performed a shoulder surgery, start by looking for orthopedic surgeons who do shoulder surgeries. Look for more than one, bearing in mind that not everyone asked to review the case will say yes and not everyone who reviews will return a favorable opinion. After an orthopedic surgeon willing to review the records is located, she will ideally be able and willing to help identify other medical issues in the case and suggest other specialties of medicine that could offer meaningful opinions on those medical issues.

Identifying an initial consulting expert for the standard of care, however, can quickly become a little more involved and a little less obvious. Consider a situation from a plaintiff's perspective: the clients are the parents of a newborn with significant birth injuries following an uneventful pregnancy. The parents believe that something was done incorrectly during the labor that led to the child's birth injuries. A plaintiff in this situation will eventually need to be able to identify whether the standard of care issues in the case stem from the nursing care or the obstetrician's care. It is entirely possible to have a birth injury case involving only one or the other or involving both. Starting the expert process by seeking review by an obstetrician is still a reasonable starting point, but it may not be enough. From the defendant's perspective, both the physician and the nursing staff should be consulted. Again, once someone is willing to look at the case, she can provide guidance to other areas of medicine that may be pertinent to the complete picture of the case.

Causation

In a medical malpractice case, the alleged deviation from the standard of care must have caused an injury that otherwise would not have occurred. The requisite causal nexus involves both but-for causation and legal or proximate cause. A plaintiff will need an expert to establish the causal link, and a defendant will need an expert to either refute the causation opinion offered by the plaintiff or offer an alternative causation theory. Importantly, the causation question is not simply whether the alleged standard of care deviation caused a harm, but rather whether it caused a harm that otherwise would not have occurred. The proffered causation expert for either side will need to have an understanding of the actual care rendered to the injured person as well as the nature of the injuries so that she can explain the means by which the care did or did not cause the injury in question.

Damages

The requisite expert(s) on damages depend on the nature and severity of the injuries, and the damages component of the case may require multiple types of experts. In a catastrophic injury case involving a brain injury to a child, damages experts would likely include a neurologist to identify the physical injury to the child, to assess the child's current functional capabilities, and to give a prognosis for future abilities or lack thereof. They would probably also include a life care planner to provide a lifetime cost analysis for all of the future needs of the child and an economist to reduce the life care plan to present value. An amputee case might add a prosthetist into the mix to offer opinions about the injured party's functional level and recommended prosthesis as well as the replacement schedule for the prosthetic limb and associated components.

Finding an Expert

There are numerous options for finding healthcare providers willing to review legal cases. A simple Internet search reveals expert witness search companies and directories where experts who are willing to review cases can post their contact information and specialties. This is one option if counsel lacks either the time or comfort level to find experts or simply feels overwhelmed by the process. Another option is word of mouth. Contact colleagues, friends, and family members—ask whether they know any good physicians or nurses in a particular medical field. The Internet also offers access to physician practice group websites and medical schools and other institutions where there are extensive CVs, bios, and e-mail addresses for physicians.

Some attorneys have strong feelings about the use of experts who advertise their medicolegal services. They view experts who advertise their legal review services as selling their opinions or being willing to say anything as long as the price is right, whereas they may perceive a nonadvertising physician within a particular specialty as more reliable, genuine, and forthright. Such attorneys might consider, however, that explaining medical concepts to a lay person (juror or judge) is not easy, and explaining opinions under the stress of effective cross-examination is a particular challenge. Physicians who frequently review cases and do work as medical experts in legal cases may be better equipped to present complicated concepts in an easy-to-understand narrative for a jury and may be better equipped to withstand cross-examination than would a physician who is not accustomed to litigation.

After developing contact information, a basic letter requesting a review is an appropriate way to begin. The letter or e-mail should introduce the lawyer, the firm, and the names of the parties and counsel involved. This basic information provides a mechanism for the potential expert to evaluate for conflicts she may have with any of the parties and lawyers. The letter should state concisely the basic issue of the case and explicitly ask whether the potential expert would be willing to review the materials (usually medical records and depositions) and offer an opinion about the care that was provided, the cause of the patient's injuries, or whatever the specific reason is for requesting review.

Throughout the process of looking for an expert to review a case, be mindful of any rules in the applicable jurisdiction concerning the basic requirements for an expert witness to be qualified to testify in a medical malpractice case. Each state will be different. In Tennessee, for example, to be qualified to testify as an expert,

> [t]he witness must be (1) "licensed to practice in the state or a contiguous bordering state," (2) [in] "a profession or specialty which would make the person's expert testimony relevant to the issues in the case," and (3) must have "had practiced this profession or specialty in one . . . of these states during the year preceding the date that the alleged injury or wrongful act occurred."[2]

Therefore, in Tennessee, a renowned expert in a given field from any state non-contiguous to Tennessee is not going to be of help. The experts themselves are unlikely to be familiar with any particular state-by-state restrictions, so be mindful of these during the expert-selection process.

Once there are experts who are willing to review the case, providing them the necessary materials is the next priority. This involves a judgment call and a balance between providing them all of the information they need to render an informed opinion in the case and the expense associated with sending volumes of records for them to review. The expense consideration is not simply the expense of accumulating and sending the records but also the hourly rate the expert is charging to review the materials. In medical malpractice cases, the records are frequently voluminous. Good organization of the records before sending them to experts for review will facilitate an easier and more cost-effective review than if experts receive a box of unorganized materials. It is also helpful to provide the expert with an organized summary of the care at issue in the case. Be mindful, however, that in many jurisdictions, correspondence with an expert is discoverable by the other side. It is thus important to assess what is said, given that the other side—and possibly the jury—may hear about it later. It may therefore be best to provide simply an organized chronological summary of the care as set forth in the medical records.

Disclosing Experts and Their Opinions

The Federal Rules of Civil Procedure are the starting point for any discussion on expert witness disclosures in federal court. If a party intends to call a witness at trial to present evidence pursuant to Federal Rules of Evidence 702, 703, or 705, the witness must be disclosed in accordance with Federal Rule of Civil Procedure 26.

2. Shipley v. Williams, 350 S.W.3d 527, 550 (Tenn. 2011) (quoting Tenn. Code Ann. § 29-26-115(b)).

The extent of the requisite disclosure may differ depending on the characterization of the witness's role in the case, but if the anticipated testimony is within Federal Rules of Evidence 702, 703, or 705, a disclosure is required.

Disclosure requirements vary in state court. The best place to start analyzing the question of what type of disclosure is required in a particular jurisdiction, however, is with the rules of evidence governing admissibility of opinion testimony and then with the rules of civil procedure governing discovery in general and, more specifically, disclosure requirements.

In federal courts, Federal Rule of Procedure 26 is the foundation for the disclosure requirements, but it implicates other rules. Expert disclosures are critical to both sides in a case because expert witnesses that have not been disclosed to the opposing side will not be permitted to testify at trial: "Under Federal Rule of Civil Procedure 37(c)(1), the appropriate sanction for failure to provide a Rule 26 disclosure is not to allow the plaintiff to use that information or witness to supply evidence on a motion, at a hearing, or at a trial."[3]

The requisite content of the expert disclosures as well as the format and timing of the disclosures is specifically set forth in Federal Rule of Civil Procedure 26(a)(2), which provides:

> (2) ***Disclosure of Expert Testimony.***
>
> (A) *In General.* In addition to the disclosures required by Rule 26(a)(1), a party must disclose to the other parties the identity of any witness it may use at trial to present evidence under Federal Rule of Evidence 702, 703, or 705.
>
> (B) *Witnesses Who Must Provide a Written Report.* Unless otherwise stipulated or ordered by the court, this disclosure must be accompanied by a written report—prepared and signed by the witness—if the witness is one retained or specially employed to provide expert testimony in the case or one whose duties as the party's employee regularly involve giving expert testimony. The report must contain:
>
> (i) a complete statement of all opinions the witness will express and the basis and reasons for them;
>
> (ii) the facts or data considered by the witness in forming them;
>
> (iii) any exhibits that will be used to summarize or support them;
>
> (iv) the witness's qualifications, including a list of all publications authored in the previous 10 years;
>
> (v) a list of all other cases in which, during the previous 4 years, the witness testified as an expert at trial or by deposition; and
>
> (vi) a statement of the compensation to be paid for the study and testimony in the case.
>
> (C) *Witnesses Who Do Not Provide a Written Report.* Unless otherwise stipulated or ordered by the court, if the witness is not required to provide a written report, this disclosure must state:

3. Daniels v. Dist. of Columbia, 15 F. Supp. 3d 62, 72 (D.D.C. 2014) (citations omitted).

(i) the subject matter on which the witness is expected to present evidence under Federal Rule of Evidence 702, 703, or 705; and
(ii) a summary of the facts and opinions to which the witness is expected to testify.

(D) *Time to Disclose Expert Testimony*. A party must make these disclosures at the times and in the sequence that the court orders. Absent a stipulation or a court order, the disclosures must be made:
(i) at least 90 days before the date set for trial or for the case to be ready for trial; or
(ii) if the evidence is intended solely to contradict or rebut evidence on the same subject matter identified by another party under Rule 26(a)(2)(B) or (C), within 30 days after the other party's disclosure.

(E) *Supplementing the Disclosure*. The parties must supplement these disclosures when required under Rule 26(e).

This rule references Federal Rule of Civil Procedure 26(a)(1), which requires initial disclosures by a party, without awaiting a discovery request, of, inter alia, the name, address, and phone number "of each individual likely to have discoverable information – along with the subjects of that information – that the disclosing party may use to support its claims of defenses, unless the use would be solely for impeachment."[4] The disclosing party must also provide a copy or description by category and location of "all documents, electronically stored information, and tangible things that the disclosing party has in its control and may use to support its claims or defenses, unless the use would be solely for impeachment."[5] With respect to damages being claimed, the disclosing party must also provide documents and other evidentiary material "unless privileged or protected from disclosure" on which the computations for damages calculations are based and "including materials bearing on the nature and extent of injuries suffered."[6]

Given the timing and sequencing of scheduling conferences, initial disclosures, and discovery under the federal rules, the initial disclosures required pursuant to Federal Rule of Civil Procedure 26(a)(1) likely will be due before decisions have been made regarding experts to be used at trial. Therefore, when preparing an expert disclosure in a federal case, be sure to include the information about that expert that would also be required pursuant to Federal Rule of Civil Procedure 26(a)(1).

With respect to the more substantive aspect of the expert's written report, the "complete statement of all opinions the witness will express and the basis and reasons for them" and "the facts or data considered by the witness in forming them" are the very heart of the disclosure. This rule requires more than a table of contents. A list of the topics the expert is expected to discuss is insufficient, and a list of the conclusions the expert is expected to reach is insufficient. The expert's

4. Fed. R. Civ. P. 26(a)(1)(A)(i).
5. Fed. R. Civ. P. 26(a)(1)(A)(ii).
6. Fed. R. Civ. P. 26(a)(1)(A)(iii).

written report under Federal Rule of Civil Procedure 26 must be a detailed statement of the testimony the witness is expected to give at trial. The most important element of Rule 26 analysis is whether the report contains a complete statement of the opinions and the basis therefor.[7] The reports must be "sufficiently detailed and complete enough to enable adequate preparation by the defendant."[8] Because the sanction for an insufficient report may be exclusion of the witness or the witness's opinions at trial, the best practice is to provide a detailed statement providing not just the expert's opinions but also the underlying basis and rationale for his opinions. The sanction for an insufficient disclosure can be fatal to a case, and therefore disclosures should be thorough.

Note that each state may have a different variation on this rule, and some local jurisdictions may have additional requirements pursuant to the local rules or even local orders of the courts. To ensure compliance with expert witness disclosure requirements in a particular jurisdiction, review not only the state's applicable rules of evidence and civil procedure but also any local rules of court and any local orders.

Disclosure of Treating Physician Opinions

Whether an opinion by a treating physician must be disclosed in advance of trial is a question of much debate. For purposes of this discussion, this section addresses two common situations: (1) the defendant healthcare provider in a medical malpractice case expressing opinions about the care he provided; and (2) a healthcare provider of the plaintiff expressing opinions about the care rendered by the defendant provider.

Per the federal rules, opinion testimony by a treating healthcare provider concerning care provided to the plaintiff would still fall within Federal Rules of Evidence 702, 703, and 705, thereby necessitating a disclosure pursuant to Federal Rule of Civil Procedure 26(a)(2). Typically in this situation, however, the healthcare provider has not been retained by either side for the purpose of providing expert testimony. The healthcare provider has simply formulated certain opinions about the patient's condition based on his care and treatment of the patient. A testifying expert must supply a written report in compliance with Federal Rule of Civil Procedure 26(a)(2)(B) only if he was specifically retained or employed to provide expert testimony in a case or if he is a party's employee with a regular duty to give expert testimony.[9]

If the expert is a treating provider who does not have to provide a written report, he must still be disclosed to the other side in compliance with

7. *See* Sharpe v. United States, 230 F.R.D. 452, 458 (E.D. Va. 2005) (citing Campbell v. McMillin, 83 F. Supp. 2d 761, 764 (S.D. Miss. 2000)).

8. *Sharpe*, 230 F.R.D. at 458.

9. Fed. R. Civ. P. 26(a)(2)(B); *see* Fielden v. CSX Transp., Inc., 482 F.3d 866, 871 (6th Cir. 2007).

Rule 26(a)(2)(C)(i)–(ii). In this situation, the disclosure required by Rule 26(a)(2)(C)(i)–(ii) is much less involved than it would be for an expert who was retained by a litigant for the purpose of providing expert opinion testimony in a case. Rule 26(a)(2) does not require a nonretained healthcare provider to provide a written report in compliance with Rule 26(a)(2)(B)(i)–(vi). Instead, counsel for the disclosing party must provide a disclosure stating "the subject matter on which the witness is expected to present evidence under Federal Rule of Evidence 702, 703, or 705; and a summary of the facts and opinions to which the witness is expected to testify."[10] "The disclosure may be made by counsel—not the expert himself—and generally may be 'considerably less extensive than the report required by Rule 26(a)(2)(B).'"[11]

In some circumstances, a treating physician's opinions to be expressed at trial may require a written report. A litigant may not simply call a treating physician to testify and elicit opinion testimony from the treating physician on any topic desirable. In deciding whether a treating physician is the type of expert that requires a written report versus only a disclosure, "[t]he determinative issue is the scope of the proposed testimony."[12]

Some federal courts allow treating physicians to offer their opinions without having provided an expert report, whereas other federal courts have not permitted this practice. The underlying basis for allowing treating physicians to testify as to their opinions without providing a written report is that it is expected that a treating healthcare provider will necessarily have to formulate opinions about the cause of a patient's condition or injury in order to treat that injury. "Determining causation may therefore be an integral part of 'treating' a patient."[13] The converse policy consideration, however, is that the courts do not want to provide a mechanism for circumventing the requirement of an expert report. In an effort to balance these considerations, some courts have "concluded that when the nature and scope of the treating physician's testimony strays from the core of the physician's treatment, Rule 26(a)(2)(B) requires the filing of an expert report from the treating physician."[14] "Under this purposive reading of Rule 26, a report is not required when a treating physician testifies within a permissive core on issues pertaining to treatment, based on what he or she learned through actual treatment and from the plaintiff's records up to and including that treatment."[15]

---

10. Fed. R. Civ. P. 26(a)(2)(C)(i)–(ii).

11. Phillips v. UAW Int'l, No. 15-10525, 2015 WL 6156968, at *1 (E.D. Mich. Oct. 19, 2015) (citing Fed. R. Civ. P. 26(a)(2) advisory committee's notes to 2010 amendments).

12. *Fielden*, 482 F.3d at 871 (quoting Wreath v. United States, 161 F.R.D. 448, 450 (D. Kan. 1995)).

13. *Fielden*, 482 F.3d at 870.

14. *Id.* at 870–71 (citing Sellers v. Butler, No. 02-3055-DJW, 2006 WL 2714274, at *4 (D. Kan. Sept. 22, 2006); Martin v. CSX Transp., Inc., 215 F.R.D. 554, 557 n.3 (S.D. Ind. 2003); Bell v. Ill. Cent. Ry. Co., No. 3:05-cv-904-DRH, 2006 WL 3841544, at *4 (S.D. Ill. Dec. 14, 2006)).

15. *Fielden*, 482 F.3d at 871.

Importantly, even federal courts differ concerning whether a treating physician may offer opinion testimony about causation without providing a written report. A majority rule and minority rule have emerged in the federal court jurisprudence, with the majority rule permitting treating physicians to offer opinion testimony on causation, diagnosis, and prognosis without the prerequisite of providing a Rule 26(a)(2)(B) report.[16]

Just like the split among the federal courts, state courts differ in their requirements on this issue. Again, knowing the prior holdings in the jurisdiction where a case is pending is critical to knowing how best to proceed relative to expert testimony disclosure requirements. Many of the cases in which these rules are being addressed are cases in which one party has moved to exclude an expert in her entirety or to exclude specific aspects of the expert's anticipated testimony due to alleged failures to comply with disclosure requirements.

Challenging the Admissibility of Experts or Aspects of Their Opinions

Parties may file pretrial motions seeking to exclude expert witnesses or specific aspects of the witnesses' anticipated testimony from trial based on failures to comply with the disclosure requirements of Rule 26. These motions may take different forms, but some common motions include motions in limine and motions for summary judgment. This section addresses a few different mechanisms for excluding an expert but focuses on the means by which a party may have an expert excluded based on the foundation of an expert's opinions.

Insufficient or Nonexistent Disclosures

Before delving into attacks on the foundation of the expert's opinions, other more basic means of excluding an expert or her opinions exist by virtue of the rules of civil procedure. Broadly speaking, most states' rules provide for discovery of expert opinions that are intended to be offered at trial and provide a means of excluding those opinions in the event that they are not disclosed. As mentioned above, the penalty under the Federal Rules of Civil Procedure for not providing a disclosure (or a sufficient disclosure) is that the witness may not testify. Additionally, if, for example, the deadline for disclosing experts is memorialized in a scheduling order, failure to comply with that order could set the stage for a motion for discovery sanctions or even dismissal pursuant to Rule of Civil Procedure 37. Rule 37 could also be used in the event that a motion to compel discovery responses to include requested information about expert witnesses had been filed and granted, but the

16. *See* McCloughan v. City of Springfield, 208 F.R.D. 236, 242 (C.D. Ill. 2002) (discussing the majority and minority rule and electing to follow the majority rule).

disclosing party has still failed to comply with the order granting the motion to compel discovery responses.[17]

As a practitioner, ensure familiarity with the various mechanisms by which a jurisdiction requires disclosure of information pertaining to expert witnesses. Under the Federal Rules of Civil Procedure, an expert disclosure is mandated even if a party has not requested such information in written discovery. In some jurisdictions, certain information about experts may be requested via pretrial discovery, and the rules governing compliance with such discovery requests are the same as they would be with any other information sought via written discovery.

Expert Witness Testimony and Daubert

In addition to rules of civil procedure imposing sanctions or penalties for a party's failure to disclose experts or respond to discovery in general, in many jurisdictions, challenges to the admissibility of an expert's opinions can also be made by attacking the foundation of the expert's opinions. The majority rule on this standard flows from *Daubert v. Merrell Dow Pharmaceuticals, Inc.*[18] and its progeny. Before *Daubert* was *Frye v. United States*[19], which set a standard for the admissibility of expert testimony essentially requiring that the methods underlying the expert's opinions be "generally accepted." This became known as the *Frye* test. The *Frye* test, however, predated the adoption of the Federal Rules of Evidence, and the Supreme Court in *Daubert* agreed that *Frye* had been superseded by the adoption of the Federal Rules of Evidence.[20] Some states, however, still follow the *Frye* test, which is the minority view, for the admissibility of expert opinion testimony. The remainder of this section, however, considers *Daubert*, which has become the majority view adopted among states.

The Background

The rules of evidence provide mechanisms for challenging the admissibility of an expert's opinions at trial. Such challenges implicate Federal Rule of Evidence 702 as well as *Daubert* and its progeny.

In the federal rules, the key rule of evidence to use in challenging the admissibility of an expert's opinions is Federal Rule of Evidence 702. The rule provides:

> A witness who is qualified as an expert by knowledge, skill, experience, training, or education may testify in the form of an opinion or otherwise if:
>
> (a) the expert's scientific, technical, or other specialized knowledge will help the trier of fact to understand the evidence or to determine a fact in issue;

17. *See, e.g.*, Tenn. R. Civ. P. 37.02.
18. Daubert v. Merrell Dow Pharm., Inc., 509 U.S. 579 (1993).
19. Frye v. United States, 293 F. 1013 (D.C. Cir. 1923).
20. *Daubert*, 509 U.S. at 587.

(b) the testimony is based on sufficient facts or data;
(c) the testimony is the product of reliable principles and methods; and
(d) the expert has reliably applied the principles and methods to the facts of the case.[21]

Parties will, from time to time, challenge the admissibility of an expert's opinions pursuant to this rule. The seminal case on this topic is *Daubert*. Generally, a proposed expert's testimony must rest on a reliable foundation and be relevant to the task at hand.[22] When faced with a challenge to the admissibility of expert testimony, the trial judge "must determine at the outset, pursuant to Rule 104(a), whether the expert is proposing to testify to (1) scientific knowledge that (2) will assist the trier of fact to understand or determine a fact in issue."[23] *Daubert* refers specifically to "scientific evidence," but subsequent to *Daubert*, the Supreme Court in the case of *Kumho Tire Co., Ltd. v. Carmichael*[24] concluded that *Daubert*'s general principle with respect to a trial court's gatekeeping function "applies to all expert testimony" as opposed to only scientific testimony.[25] *Kumho Tire* confirmed that the principles set forth in *Daubert* included technical or other specialized knowledge, which is consistent with the current language in Federal Rules of Evidence 702.

Although the courts have not established an exhaustive list of factors to be considered in determining the admissibility of expert testimony pursuant to Rule 702, considerations listed by the Supreme Court of the United States in *Daubert* include whether the scientific technique has been or can be tested, whether the theory or technique has been subjected to peer review and publication, and the known or potential rate of error, as well as the existence and maintenance of standards controlling the technique's operation in the case of a particular scientific technique and the general acceptance within the scientific community.[26] The court's focus of the inquiry "must be solely on principles and methodology, not on the conclusions that they generate."[27] With respect to these *Daubert* factors, the Supreme Court in *Kumho Tire* observed that trial judges have broad latitude in determining whether the *Daubert* factors are reasonable measures of an expert's reliability in a particular case.[28] Cases post–*Kumho Tire* have considered and adopted other factors beyond just the *Daubert* factors for evaluating the relevance and reliability of expert opinions based on technical and other specialized knowledge.

Specifically in the context of medical malpractice cases, a few examples of challenges to the reliability of expert opinions have included

21. Fed. R. Evid. 702.
22. *See id.*; *Daubert*, 509 U.S. 579.
23. *Daubert*, 509 U.S. at 592.
24. Kumho Tire Co., Ltd. v. Carmichael, 526 U.S. 137 (1999).
25. *Id.* at 147.
26. *Daubert*, 509 U.S. at 593–94.
27. *Id.* at 595.
28. *Kumho Tire Co.*, 526 U.S. 137.

- causation opinions about the time frame within which care and treatment needed to be rendered to reduce neurological damage that were too vague to assist the trier of fact; had no support in any empirical data, survey, study, or literature; and were based on a theory that the expert had not tested and that had no associated error rate;[29]
- standard of care opinions based on incorrect factual assertions;[30] and
- causation opinions not supported by the literature that was cited in support of them.[31]

In *McDowell v. Brown*,[32] the court noted that "an expert opinion is inadmissible when the only connection between the conclusion and the existing data is the expert's own assertions . . . ."[33] The court excluded an expert in the case because the expert conceded that his causation theory lacked empirical evidence or scientific support, and he acknowledged there were no studies that assessed the effect of surgery on the neurological condition at issue at various points in time. The expert acknowledged that he was unable to quantify what the plaintiff's condition would have been had surgery been performed earlier. This expert actually testified that he was relying on medical logic and acknowledged he lacked proof for his logic theory. The court noted that *Daubert* would allow an expert to draw conclusions from existing data, but in this case the expert drew conclusions in the absence of any existing data. This testimony did not satisfy the requirements of Rule 702 and was properly excluded.

Another expert on causation in *McDowell* was excluded on similar grounds. He acknowledged that his causation theory had not been tested, subjected to peer review, or assigned a rate of error. These opinions did not satisfy *Daubert*'s reliability requirement and were excluded.[34] The court in *McDowell* summarized the plaintiff's causation opinions as boiling down to an opinion that earlier intervention would be preferable and then making a leap from this theory to the theory that the specific delay in the case caused the plaintiff's injury. The court stressed that the proffered experts could not point to any existing data or research detailing the extent of injury or recovery and different time intervals.[35] The court excluded all of these expert opinions.

In *Berk v. St. Vincent's Hospital & Medical Center*, the plaintiff's proffered expert opinion was based on a factual assumption that was contradictory to the plaintiff's deposition testimony about the events in question.[36] The expert report for this proffered expert also included factual inaccuracies about the dates when cer-

---

29. McDowell v. Brown, 392 F.3d 1283 (11th Cir. 2004).
30. Berk v. St. Vincent's Hosp. & Med. Ctr., 380 F. Supp. 2d 334 (S.D.N.Y. 2005).
31. Sullivan v. U.S. Dep't of Navy, 365 F.3d 827 (9th Cir. 2004).
32. *McDowell*, 392 F.3d 1283.
33. *Id.* at 1300.
34. *Id.* at 1301.
35. *Id.*
36. Berk v. St. Vincent's Hosp. & Med. Ctr., 380 F. Supp. 2d 334, 351–52 (S.D.N.Y. 2005).

tain of the plaintiff's symptoms were reported to the defendant physician as well as inaccurate dates about when the plaintiff contacted the physician. The expert acknowledged in his deposition that he had not reviewed the deposition of the plaintiff or of any of the other parties or witnesses in the case before developing his expert opinion.[37] The court concluded that the expert's report and deposition testimony "failed the *Daubert* reliability test" and that there was "simply too great an analytical gap between the data and the opinion proffered by [the expert]" for the opinion about the defendant having committed medical malpractice to be admissible.[38]

In *Sullivan v. U.S. Department of Navy,*[39] one issue was whether the length of a surgery caused a subsequent wound infection. The district court found that the plaintiff's expert's causation theory was unsupported by the scientific literature provided by the plaintiff and therefore excluded the opinions. This deprived the plaintiff of any causation proof in her case, and summary judgment was therefore awarded to the defendant.[40]

On appeal, the Ninth Circuit observed that the district court applied only the *Daubert* standard, but the expert's opinion was subject to the *Daubert-Kumho* criteria requiring the testimony to be both reliable and relevant.[41] The Ninth Circuit considered the expert's opinions as well as the literature she cited in support of those opinions. The Ninth Circuit felt that the district court was expecting the literature to state the precise amount of the increased risk of infection. The court held that "the district court abused its discretion and invaded the province of the expert by requiring the texts to state the precise type of harm explained by the specialized testimony of a medical expert."[42] The Ninth Circuit reversed, finding the exclusion of the expert's opinions to be error because the expert's testimony was "based on specialized as distinguished from scientific knowledge, [and therefore] the *Daubert* factors are not intended to be exhaustive or unduly restrictive."[43]

Although these three cases are far from an exhaustive list of examples of circumstances in medical malpractice that may or may not lend themselves to *Daubert* challenges, they offer some context for use of such challenges. Certainly the experts in *McDowell* were lacking considerable support for the opinions they were advancing, and the court was not persuaded by the use of "medical logic." The court in *Berk* was clearly troubled by the expert's numerous factual inaccuracies and complete failure to apprise himself of the facts by reviewing the depositions. When deciding what material to send to consulting experts, consider erring on the side of caution and providing everything possibly pertinent to the expert's opinion. A detailed discussion of the facts involved in a particular case should be

37. *Id.* at 353.
38. *Id.*
39. Sullivan v. U.S. Dep't of Navy, 365 F.3d 827 (9th Cir. 2004).
40. *Id.* at 832.
41. *Id.* at 833.
42. *Id.* at 834.
43. *Id.*

had with the expert even before finalizing the expert's disclosure, and certainly a refresher conversation should be had in preparation for the expert's deposition.

Considerations

When deciding whether to make a *Daubert* challenge, there are multiple considerations. These include the likelihood of success, the strategic timing of a motion, and the mechanism of filing the motion. In terms of likelihood of success, this is not simply a matter of the perceived strength of the motion based on the expert's lack of support for his opinions but is also based on how the courts in a particular jurisdiction routinely treat these motions. Local research concerning the frequency of such motions, the grounds most often articulated for such motions, and the rulings of the local courts would be prudent.

Another consideration is the timing of the motion. Is there enough information via the expert's disclosure to support a challenge upon receipt of the disclosure? Is a discovery deposition of the expert necessary to explore the expert's underlying basis for his opinions? Depending on the precise nature of the challenge, voir dire at trial may even be necessary before being able to fully attack the foundation for the expert's opinions.

With respect to the mechanism of pursuing such a challenge, this could be done via a motion in limine, a motion for summary judgment, or a preliminary hearing pursuant to Rule of Evidence 104(a).

The Process

Challenging an expert based on the underlying foundation for his opinions can be done via a motion in limine prior to trial, a motion for summary judgment, or a preliminary hearing pursuant to Rule of Evidence 104(a). A motion in limine would seek to exclude the expert or the expert's opinions because of some deficiency in the underlying basis or reliability of the opinions. A motion in limine could include an argument rooted in Rule of Evidence 104(a). A motion in limine could also be used to exclude an expert for failure of a party to have properly disclosed the expert within the time allowed pursuant to a scheduling order or to exclude a disclosed expert who does not meet the competency requirements for experts in the particular jurisdiction.

A motion for summary judgment still challenges the underlying basis or reliability of the expert but takes the result a step further: if the defendant is able to exclude the plaintiff's experts in a medical malpractice case, then the plaintiff cannot meet his burden of proof, and the defendant is entitled to summary judgment.[44] A preliminary hearing pursuant to Rule of Evidence 104(a) would involve the same challenges to the foundation of the expert's opinions. If the motion for

44. For an example of a challenge asserted in the context of a summary judgment motion, see *McDowell v. Brown*, 392 F.3d 1283 (11th Cir. 2004).

preliminary hearing is the only motion filed and is granted, it may need to then be followed by a motion for summary judgment if the granting of the motion for preliminary hearing then precludes the plaintiff from being able to establish his prima facie case. The applicable rules for each of these mechanisms as well as their various implications on a case should be evaluated on a case-by-case basis because no one mechanism is right for every case.

Conclusion

Expert witnesses are critical to a medical malpractice or healthcare liability case for both the plaintiff and the defendant. The practical and legal considerations involved in finding, retaining, disclosing, presenting, and challenging expert witnesses are lengthy. The time period from identifying the types of experts needed through the actual crafting of a disclosure can be extremely burdensome due to time constraints on both the lawyer and the expert, so start the process early upon receipt of a case. Tackling the expert witness component of a case in deliberate steps should aid in alleviating some of the anxiety that can come with the process.

Table of Cases

Index